Prisoner for Blasphemy

G. W. Foote

Prisoner for Blasphemy

Copyright © 2020 Bibliotech Press
All rights reserved

The present edition is a reproduction of previous publication of this classic work. Minor typographical errors may have been corrected without note, however, for an authentic reading experience the spelling, punctuation, and capitalization have been retained from the original text.

ISBN: 978-1-64799-374-0

CONTENTS

	PREFACE	iv
CHAPTER I	THE STORM BREWING	1
CHAPTER II	OUR FIRST SUMMONS	8
CHAPTER III	MR BRADLAUGH INCLUDED	14
CHAPTER IV	OUR INDICTMENT	21
CHAPTER V	ANOTHER PROSECUTION	28
CHAPTER VI	PREPARING FOR TRIAL	37
CHAPTER VII	AT THE OLD BAILEY	45
CHAPTER VIII	NEWGATE	61
CHAPTER IX	THE SECOND TRIAL	72
CHAPTER X	"BLACK MARIA"	80
CHAPTER XI	HOLLOWAY GAOL	87
CHAPTER XII	PRISON LIFE	94
CHAPTER XIII	PARSON PLAFORD	108
CHAPTER XIV	THE THIRD TRIAL	117
CHAPTER XV	LOSS AND GAIN	127
CHAPTER XVI	A LONG NIGHT	133
CHAPTER XVII	DAYLIGHT	138

PREFACE

This little volume tells a strange and painful story; strange, because the experiences of a prisoner for blasphemy are only known to three living Englishmen; and painful, because their unmerited sufferings are a sad reflection on the boasted freedom of our age.

My own share in this misfortune is all I could pretend to describe with fidelity. Without (I hope) any meretricious display of fine writing, I have related the facts of my case, giving a precise account of my prosecutions, and as vivid a narrative as memory allows of my imprisonment in Holloway Gaol. I have striven throughout to be truthful and accurate, nothing extenuating, nor setting down aught in malice; and I have tried to hit the happy mean between negligence and prolixity. Whether or not I have succeeded in the second respect the reader must be the judge; and if he cannot be so in the former respect, he will at least be able to decide whether the writer means to be candid and bears the appearance of honesty.

One reason why I have striven to be exact is that my record may be of service to the future historian of our time. It is always rash to appeal to the future, as a posturing English novelist did in one of his Prefaces; and it is well to remember the witticism of Voltaire, who, on hearing an ambitious poeticule read his Ode to Posterity, doubted whether it would reach its address. But it is the facts, and not my personality, that are important in this case. My trial will be a conspicuous event in the history of the struggle for religious freedom, and in consequence of Lord Coleridge's and Sir James Stephen's utterances, it may be of considerable moment in the history of the Criminal Law. It is more than possible that I shall be the last prisoner for blasphemy in England. That alone is a circumstance of distinction, which gives my story a special character, quite apart from my individuality. As a muddle-headed acquaintance said, intending to be complimentary, Some men are born to greatness, others achieve it, and I had it thrust upon me.

Prosecutions for Blasphemy have not been frequent. Sir James Stephen was able to record nearly all of them in his "History of the Criminal Law." The last before mine occurred in 1857, when Thomas Pooley, a poor Cornish well-sinker, was sentenced by the late Mr. Justice Coleridge to twenty months' imprisonment for chalking some "blasphemous" words on a gate-post. Fortunately this monstrous punishment excited public indignation. Mill, Buckle, and other eminent men, interested themselves in the case, and Pooley was released after undergoing a quarter of his sentence. From that time until my prosecution, that is for nearly a whole generation, the odious law was allowed to slumber, although tons of "blasphemy" were published every year. This long desuetude induced Sir James Stephen, in his "Digest of the Criminal Law" to regard it as "practically obsolete." But the event has proved that no law is obsolete until it is repealed. It has also proved Lord Coleridge's observation that there is, in the case of some laws, a "discriminating laxity," as well as Professor Hunter's remark that the Blasphemy Laws survive as a dangerous weapon in the hands of any fool or fanatic who likes to set them in motion.

In the pamphlet entitled Blasphemy No Crime, which I published during my prosecution, and which is still in print if anyone is curious to see it, I contended that Blasphemy is only our old friend Heresy in disguise, and that, we know, is a priestly manufacture. My view has since been borne out by two high authorities. Lord Coleridge says that "this law of blasphemous libel first appears in our books—at least the cases relating to it are first reported—shortly after the curtailment or abolition of the jurisdiction of the Ecclesiastical Courts in matters temporal. Speaking broadly, before the time of Charles II. these things would have been dealt with as heresy; and the libellers so-called of more recent days would have suffered as heretics in earlier times." [Reference: The Law of Blasphemous Libel. The Summing-up in the case of Regina v. Foote and others. Revised with a Preface by the Lord Chief Justice of England. London, Stevens and Sons.] Sir James Stephen also, after referring to the writ De Heretico Comburendo, under which heresy and blasphemy were punishable by burning alive, and which was abolished in 1677, without abridging the jurisdiction of Ecclesiastical Courts "in cases of atheism, blasphemy, heresie, or schism, and other damnable doctrines and opinions," adds that "In this state of things, the Court of Queen's Bench took upon itself some of the functions of the old Courts of Star Chamber and High Commission, and treated as misdemeanours at common law many things which those courts had formerly punished... This was the origin of the modern law as to blasphemy and blasphemous libel." [Reference: Blasphemy and Blasphemous Libel. By Sir James Stephen. Fortnightly Review, March, 1884.]

Less than ten years after the "glorious revolution" of 1688

there was passed a statute, known as the 9 and 10 William III., c. 32, and called "An Act for the more effectual suppressing of Blasphemy and Profaneness." This enacts that "any person or persons having been educated in, or at any time having made profession of, the Christian religion within this realm who shall, by writing, printing, teaching, or advised speaking, deny any one of the persons in the Holy Trinity to be God, or shall assert or maintain there are more gods than one, or shall deny the Christian doctrine to be true, or the Holy Scriptures of the Old and New Testament to be of divine authority," shall upon conviction be disabled from holding any ecclesiastical, civil, or military employment, and on a second conviction be imprisoned for three years and deprived for ever of all civil rights.

Lord Coleridge and Sir James Stephen call this statute "ferocious," but as it is still unrepealed there is no legal reason why it should not be enforced. Curiously, however, the reservation which was inserted to protect the Jews has frustrated the whole purpose of the Act; at any rate, there never has been a single prosecution under it. So much of the statute as affected the Unitarians was ostensibly repealed by the 53 George III., c. 160. But Lord Eldon in 1817 doubted whether it was ever repealed at all; and so late as 1867 Chief Baron Kelly and Lord Bramwell, in the Court of Exchequer, held that a lecture on "The Character and Teachings of Christ: the former defective, the latter misleading" was an offence against the statute. It is not so clear, therefore, that Unitarians are out of danger; especially as the judges have held that this Act was special, without in any way affecting the common law of Blasphemy, under which all prosecutions have been conducted.

Dr. Blake Odgers, however, thinks the Unitarians are perfectly safe, and he has informed them so in a memorandum on the Blasphemy Laws drawn up at their request. This gentleman has a right to his opinion, but no Unitarian of any courage will be proud of his advice. He deliberately recommends the body to which he belongs to pay no attention to the Blasphemy Laws, and to lend no assistance to the agitation for repealing them, on the ground that when you are safe yourself it is Quixotic to trouble about another man's danger; which is, perhaps, the most cowardly and contemptible suggestion that could be made. Several Unitarians were burnt in Elizabeth's reign, two were burnt in the reign of James I., and one narrowly escaped hanging under the Commonwealth. The whole body was excluded from the Toleration Act of 1688, and included in the Blasphemy Act of William III. But

Unitarians have since yielded the place of danger to more advanced bodies, and they may congratulate themselves on their safety; but to make their own safety a reason for conniving at the persecution of others is a depth of baseness which Dr. Blake Odgers has fathomed, though happily without persuading the majority of his fellows to descend to the same ignominy.

It will be observed that the Act specifies certain heterodox opinions as blasphemous, and says nothing as to the language in which they may be couched. Evidently the crime lay not in the manner, but in the matter. The Common Law has always held the same view, and my Indictment, like that of all my predecessors, charged me with bringing the Holy Scriptures and the Christian religion "into disbelief and contempt." With all respect to Lord Coleridge's authority, I cannot but think that Sir James Stephen is right in maintaining that the crime of blasphemy consists in the expression of certain opinions, and that it is only an aggravation of the crime to express them in "offensive" language.

Judge North, on my first trial, plainly told the jury that any denial of the existence of Deity or of Providence was blasphemy; although on my second trial, in order to procure a conviction, he narrowed his definition to "any contumelious or profane scoffing at the Holy Scriptures or the Christian religion." It is evident, therefore, what his lordship believes the law to be. With a certain order of minds it is best to deal sharply; their first statements are more likely to be true than their second. For the rest, Judge North is unworthy of consideration. It is remarkable that, although he charged the jury twice in my case, Sir James Stephen does not regard his views as worth a mention.

Lord Coleridge says the law of blasphemy "is undoubtedly a disagreeable law," and in my opinion he lets humanity get the better of his legal judgment. He lays it down that "if the decencies of controversy are observed, even the fundamentals of religion may be attacked without a person being guilty of blasphemous libel."

Now such a decision can only be a stepping-stone to the abolition of the law. Who can define "the decencies of controversy?" Everyone has his own criterion in such matters, which is usually unconscious and fluctuating. What shocks one man pleases another. Does not the proverb say that one man's meat is another man's poison? Lord Coleridge reduces Blasphemy to a matter of taste, and de gustibus non est disputandum. According to this view, the prosecution has simply to put any heretical work into the hands of a jury, and say, "Gentlemen, do you like that? If you do, the prisoner is innocent; if you do not, you must find him guilty." Such a law puts a rope round the neck of every writer who soars above commonplace, or has any gift of wit or humor. It hands over the discussion of all important topics to pedants and blockheads, and bans the argumentum ad absurdum which has been employed by all the great satirists from Aristophanes to Voltaire.

When Bishop South was reproached by an Episcopal brother for being witty in the pulpit, he replied, "My dear brother in the Lord, do you mean to say that if God had given you any wit you wouldn't have used it?" Let Bishop South stand for the "blasphemer," and his dull brother for the orthodox jury, and you have the moral at once.

"Such a law," says Sir James Stephen, "would never work." You cannot really distinguish between substance and style; you must either forbid or permit all attacks on Christianity. Great religious and political changes are never made by calm and moderate language. Was any form of Christianity ever substituted either for Paganism or any other form of Christianity without heat, exaggeration, and fierce invective? Saint Augustine ridiculed one of the Roman gods in grossly indecent language. Men cannot discuss doctrines like eternal punishment as they do questions in philology. And "to say that you may discuss the truth of religion, but that you may not hold up its doctrines to contempt, ridicule, or indignation, is either to take away with one hand what you concede with the other, or to confine the discussion to a small and in many ways uninfluential class of persons." Besides, Sir James Stephen says,

> "There is one reflection which seems to me to prove with conclusive force that the law upon this subject can be explained and justified only on what I regard as its true principle—the principle of persecution. It is that if the law were really impartial, and punished blasphemy only because it offends the feelings of believers, it ought also to punish such preaching as offends the feelings of unbelievers. All the more earnest and enthusiastic forms of religion are extremely offensive to those who do not believe them. Why should not people who are not Christians be protected against the rough, coarse, ignorant ferocity with which they are often told that they and theirs are on the way to hell-fire for ever and ever? Such a doctrine, though necessary to be known if true, is, if false, revolting and mischievous to the last degree. If the law in no degree recognised these doctrines as true, if it were as neutral as the Indian Penal Code is between Hindoos and Mohametans, it would have to apply to the Salvation Army the same rule as it applies to the Freethinker and its contributors."

Excellently put. I argued in the same way, though perhaps less tersely, in my defence. I pointed out that there is no law to protect the "decencies of controversy" in any but religious discussions, and this exception can only be defended on the ground that Christianity is true and must not be attacked. But Lord Coleridge holds that it may be attacked. How then can he ask that it shall only be attacked in polite language? And if Freethinkers must only strike with kid gloves, why are Christians allowed to use not only the naked fist, but knuckle-dusters, bludgeons, and daggers? In the war of ideas, any party which imposes restraints on others to which it does not subject itself, is guilty of persecution; and the finest phrases, and the most dexterous special pleading, cannot alter the fact.

Sir James Stephen holds that the Blasphemy Laws are concerned with the matter of publications, that "a large part of the most serious and most important literature of the day is illegal," and that every book-seller who sells, and everyone who lends to his friend, a copy of Comte's Positive Philosophy, or of Renan's Vie de Jesus, commits a crime punishable with fine and imprisonment. Sir James Stephen dislikes the law profoundly, but he prefers "stating it in its natural naked deformity to explaining it away in such a manner as to prolong its existence and give it an air of plausibility and humanity." To terminate this mischievous law he has drafted a Bill, which many Liberal members of Parliament have promised to support, and which will soon be introduced. Its text is as follows:

"Whereas certain laws now in force and intended for the promotion of religion are no longer suitable for that purpose and it is expedient to repeal them,
"Be it enacted as follows:

"1. After the passing of this Act no criminal proceedings shall be instituted in any Court whatever, against any person whatever, for Atheism, blasphemy at common law, blasphemous libel, heresy, or schism, except only criminal proceedings instituted in Ecclesiastical Courts against clergymen of the Church of England.

"2. An Act passed in the first year of his late Majesty King Edward VI., c. 1, intituled 'An Act against such as shall unreverently speak against the sacrament of the body and blood of Christ, commonly called the sacrament of the altar, and for the receiving thereof in both kinds,' and an Act passed in the 9th and 10th year of his late Majesty King William III., c. 35, intituled an Act for the more effectual suppressing of blasphemy and profaneness are hereby repealed.

"3. Provided that nothing herein contained shall be deemed to affect the provisions of an Act passed in the nineteenth year of his late Majesty King George II., c. 21, intituled 'An Act more effectually to prevent profane cursing and swearing,' or any other provision of any other Act of Parliament not hereby expressly repealed."

Until this Bill is carried no heterodox writer is safe. Sir James Stephen's view of the law may be shared by other judges, and if a bigot sat on the bench he might pass a heavy sentence on a distinguished "blasphemer." Let it not be said that their manner is so different from mine that no jury would convict; for when I read extracts from Clifford, Swinburne, Maudsley, Matthew Arnold, James Thomson, Lord Amberley, Huxley, and other heretics whose works are circulated by Mudie, Lord Coleridge remarked "I confess, as I heard them, I had, and have a difficulty in distinguishing them from the alleged libels. They do appear to me to be open to the same charge, on the same grounds, as Mr. Foote's writings."

Personally I understand the Blasphemy Laws well enough. They are the last relics of religious persecution. What Lord Coleridge read from Starkie as the law of blasphemous libel, I regard with Sir James Stephen as "flabby verbiage." Lord Coleridge is himself a master of style, and I suppose his admiration of Starkie's personal character has blinded his judgment. Starkie simply raises a cloud of words to hide the real nature of the Blasphemy Laws. He shows how Freethinkers may be punished without avowing the principle of persecution. Instead of frankly saying that Christianity must not be attacked, he imputes to aggressive heretics "a malicious and mischievous intention," and "apathy and indifference to the interests of society;" and he justifies their being punished, not for their actions, but for their motives: a principle which, if it were introduced into our jurisprudence, would produce a chaos.

Could there be a more ridiculous assumption than that a man who braves obloquy, social ostracism, and imprisonment for his principles, is indifferent to the interest of society? Let Christianity strike Freethinkers if it will, but why add insult to injury? Why brand us as cowards when you martyr us? Why charge us with hypocrisy when we dare your hate?

Persecution, like superstition, dies hard, but it dies. What though I have suffered the heaviest punishment inflicted on a Freethinker for a hundred and twenty years? Is not the night always darkest and coldest before the dawn? Is not the tiger's dying spring most fierce and terrible?

My sufferings, therefore, are not without the balm of consolation. I see that the future is already brightening with a new hope. Without rising to the supreme height of Danton, who cried "Let my name be blighted that France be free," I feel a humbler pleasure in reflecting that I may have been instrumental in breaking the last fetter on the freedom of the press.

G. W. FOOTE

February 1st, 1886

CHAPTER I
THE STORM BREWING

In the merry month of May, 1881, I started a paper called the Freethinker, with the avowed object of waging "relentless war against Superstition in general and the Christian Superstition in particular." I stated in the first paragraph of the first number that this new journal would have a new policy; that it would "do its best to employ the resources of Science, Scholarship, Philosophy and Ethics against the claims of the Bible as a Divine Revelation," and that it would "not scruple to employ for the same purpose any weapons of ridicule or sarcasm that might be borrowed from the armoury of Common Sense."

As the Freethinker was published at the people's price of a penny, and was always edited in a lively style, with a few short articles and plenty of racy paragraphs, it succeeded from the first; and becoming well known, not through profuse advertisement, but through the recommendation of its readers, its circulation increased every week. Within a year of its birth it had outdistanced all its predecessors. No Freethought journal ever progressed with such amazing rapidity. True, this was largely due to the fact that the Freethought party had immensely increased in numbers; but much of it was also due to the policy of the paper, which supplied, as the advertising gentry say, "a long-felt want." Although the first clause of its original programme was never wholly forgotten, we gradually paid the greatest attention to the second, indulging more and more in Ridicule and Sarcasm, and more and more cultivating Common Sense. A dangerous policy, as I was sometimes warned; but for that very reason all the more necessary. The more Bigotry writhed and raged, the more I felt that our policy was telling. Borrowing a metaphor from Carlyle's "Frederick," I likened Superstition to the boa, which defies all ponderous assaults, and will not yield to the pounding of sledge-hammers, but sinks dead when some expert thrusts in a needle's point and punctures the spinal column.

I had a further incentive. Mr. Bradlaugh's infamous treatment by the bigots had revolutionised my ideas of Freethought policy. Although never timid, I was until then practically ignorant of the horrible spirit of persecution; and with the generous enthusiasm of youth I fondly imagined that the period of combat was ended, that the liberty of platform and press was finally won, that

Supernaturalism was hopelessly scotched although obviously not slain, and that Freethinkers should now devote themselves to cultivating the fields they had won instead of raiding into the enemy's territory. Alas for the illusions of hope! They were rudely dispelled by a few "scenes" in the House of Commons, and barred from all chance of re-gathering by the wild display of intolerance outside. I saw, in quite another sense than Garth Wilkinson's, the profound truth of his saying that—

> "The Duke of Wellington's advice, Do not make a little war, is
> applicable to internal conflicts against evil in society. For
> little wars have no background of resources, they do not know
> the strength of the enemy, and the peace that follows them for
> the most part leaves the evil in dispute nearly its whole territory;
> perhaps is purchased by guaranteeing the evil by treaty; and
> leaves the case of offence more difficult of attack by reason
> of concession to wrong premises."
> ("Human Science and Divine Revelation," Preface, p. vi.)

Yes, the war with Superstition must be fought a outrance. We must decline either treaty or truce. I hold that the one great work of our time is the destruction of theology, the immemorial enemy of mankind, which has wasted in the chase of chimeras very much of the world's best intellect, fatally perverted our moral sentiments, fomented discord and division, supported all the tyranny of privilege and sanctioned all debasement of the people. Far be it from me to argue this point with any dissident. I prefer to leave him to the logic of events, which has convinced me, and may some day convince him.

But to recur. Before the Freethinker had reached its third number I began to reflect on the advisability of illustrating it, and bringing in the artist's pencil to aid the writer's pen. I soon resolved to do this, and the third and fourth numbers contained a woodcut on the front page. In the fifth number there appeared an exquisite little burlesque sketch of the Calling of Samuel, by a skilful artist whose name I cannot disclose. Although not ostensibly, it was actually, the first of those Comic Bible Sketches for which the Freethinker afterwards became famous; and from that date, with the exception of occasional intervals due to difficulties there is no need to explain, my little paper was regularly illustrated. During the whole twelve months of my imprisonment the illustrations were discontinued by my express order. I was not averse to their appearing, but I knew the terrible obstacles and dangers my temporary successor would have to meet, and I left him a written prohibition of them, which he was free to publish, in order to shield him against the possible charge of cowardice. Since my release from prison they have been resumed, and they will be continued until I go to prison again, unless I see some better reason than Christian menace for their cessation.

The same fifth number of the Freethinker contained an account of the first part of "La Bible Amusante," issued by the Anti-Clerical publishing house in the Rue des Ecoles. That notice was from my own pen, and I venture to reprint the opening paragraphs.

> "Voltaire's method of attacking Christianity has always approved itself to French Freethinkers. They regard the statement that he treated religious questions in a spirit of levity as the weak defence of those who know that irony and sarcasm are the deadliest enemies of their faith. Superstition dislikes argument, but it hates laughter. Nimble and far-flashing wit is more potent against error than the slow dull logic of the schools; and the great humorists and wits of the world have done far more to clear its head and sweeten its heart than all its sober philosophers from Aristotle to Kant.
>
> "We in England have Comic Histories, Comic Geographies, and Comic Grammars, but a Comic Bible would horrify us. At sight of such blasphemy Bumble would stand aghast, and Mrs. Grundy would scream with terror. But Bumble and Mrs. Grundy are less important personages in France, and so the country of Rabelais and Voltaire produces what we are unable to tolerate in thought."

I concluded by saying—"We shall introduce the subsequent numbers to the attention of our readers, and, if possible, we shall reproduce in the Freethinker some of the raciest plates. We shall be greeted with shrieks of pious wrath if we do so, but we are not easily frightened."

There was really more than editorial fashion in this "we," for at that time Mr. Ramsey was half proprietor of the Freethinker, and his consent had of course to be obtained before I could undertake such a dangerous enterprise. I gladly avow that he showed no hesitation; on the contrary, he heartily fell in with the project. He frankly left the editorial conduct of our paper in my hands, despised the accusation of Blasphemy, and defied its law. His half-proprietorship of the Freethinker has terminated, but we still work together in our several ways for the cause of Freethought. Mr. Ramsey went with me into the furnace of persecution, and he bore his sufferings with manly fortitude.

The Freethinker steadily progressed in circulation, and in January, 1882, I was able to secure the services of my old friend, Joseph Mazzini Wheeler, as sub-editor. He had for long years contributed gratuitously to my literary ventures, and those who ever turn over a file of the Secularist or the Liberal will see with what activity he wielded his trenchant pen. When he became my paid sub-editor, our relations remained unchanged. We worked as loyal colleagues for a cause we both loved, and treated as a mere accident the fact of my being his principal. The same feeling animates us still, nor do I think it can ever suffer alteration.

The new year's number, dated January 1, 1882, referred to Mr. Wheeler's accession, and to that of Dr. Edward Aveling, who then became a member of the regular staff. It also referred to the policy of the Freethinker, and to another subject of the gravest interest—namely, the threats of prosecution which had appeared in several Christian journals. As "pieces of justification," to use a French phrase, I quote these two passages:

"Our ill-wishers (what journal has none?) have been of two kinds. In the first place, the Christians, disgusted with our "blasphemy," predicted a speedy failure. The wish was father to the thought. These latter-day prophets were just as false as their predecessors. Now that they witness our indisputable success, they shake their heads, look at us askance, mutter something like curses, and pray the Lord to turn us from our evil ways. One or two bigots, more than ordinarily foolish, have threatened to suppress us with the strong arm of the law. We defy them to do their worst. We have no wish to play the martyr, but we should not object to take a part in dragging the monster of persecution into the light of day, even at the cost of some bites and scratches. As the Freethinker was intended to be a fighting organ, the savage hostility of the enemy is its best praise. We mean to incur their hatred more and more. The war with superstition should be ruthless. We ask no quarter and we shall give none.

"Secondly, we have had to encounter the dislike of mealy-mouthed Freethinkers, who want omelettes without breaking of eggs and revolutions without shedding of blood. They object to ridiculing people who say that twice two are five. They even resent a dogmatic statement that twice two are four. Perhaps they think four and a half a very fair compromise. Now this is recreancy to truth, and therefore to progress. No great cause was ever won by the half-hearted. Let us be faithful to our convictions, and shun paltering in a double sense. Truth, as Renan says, can dispense with politeness; and while we shall never stoop to personal slander or innuendo, we shall assail error without tenderness or mercy. And if, as we believe, ridicule is the most potent weapon against superstition, we shall not scruple to use it."

These extracts from my old manifestoes may possess little other value, but they at least show this, that the peculiar policy of the Freethinker was not adopted in a moment of levity, but was from the first deliberately pursued; and that while I held on the even tenor of my way, I was fully conscious of its dangers.

Early in January there fell into my hands a copy of a circular to Members of Parliament by Henry Varley, the Notting Hill revivalist. This person was a notorious trader in scandal, and he still pursues that avocation. Many of his discourses are "delivered to men only," an advertisement which is sure to attract a large audience; and one of them, which he has published, is just on a level with the quack publications that are thrust into young men's hands in the street. Henry Varley had already issued one private circular about Mr. Bradlaugh, full of the most brazen falsehoods and the grossest defamation; and containing, as it did, garbled extracts from Mr. Bradlaugh's writings, and artfully-manipulated quotations from books he had never written or published, it undoubtedly did him a serious injury. The new circular was worthy of the author of the first. It was addressed "To the Members of the House of Commons," and was "for private circulation only." The indignant butcher, for that is his trade, wished "to submit to their notice the horrible blasphemies that are appended, and quoted from a new weekly publication issued from the office where Mr. Bradlaugh's weekly journal, the National Reformer, is published. The paper is entitled the Freethinker, and is edited by G. W. Foote, one of Mr. Bradlaugh's prominent supporters, and one of his right hand men at the Hall of Science." The Commons of England were also requested to notice that "Dr. Aveling, who for some years has been one of Mr. Bradlaugh's chief helpers, is another contributor to this disgraceful product of Atheism." In conclusion, they were called upon to "devise means to stay this hideous prostitution of the liberty of the Press, by making these shameless blasphemers amenable to the existing law."

It is a curious thing that such a fervid champion of religion should always attack unbelievers with private circulars. Yet this is the policy that Henry Varley has always pursued. He is a religious bravo, who lurks in the dark, and strikes at Freethinkers with a poisoned dagger. More than once he has flooded Northampton with the foulest libels on Mr. Bradlaugh, invariably issued without the printer's name, in open violation of the law. He is liable for a fine of five pounds for every copy circulated, but the action must be initiated by the Attorney-General, and our Christian Government refuses to punish when the offence is committed by one of their own creed, and the sufferer is only an Atheist.

Varley's circular served its evil purpose, for soon after

Parliament assembled in February, Mr. C. K. Freshfield, member for Dover, asked the Home Secretary whether the Government intended to prosecute the Freethinker.

Sir William Harcourt gave the following reply:

"I am sorry to say my attention has been called to a paper bearing the title of the Freethinker, published in Northampton, and I agree that nothing can be more pernicious to the minds of right-thinking people than publications of that description— (cheers)—but I think it has been the view for a great many years of all persons responsible in these matters, that more harm than advantage is produced to public morals by Government prosecutions in cases of this kind. (Hear, hear). I believe they are better left to the reprobation which they will meet in this country from all decent members of society. (Cheers)."

This highly disingenuous answer was characteristic of the member for Derby. His reference to the Freethinker as published at Northampton, clearly proves that he had never seen it; and his unctuous allusions to "public morals" and "decent members of society" are further evidence in the same direction. The Freethinker was accused of blasphemy, but until Sir William Harcourt gave the cue not even its worst enemies charged it with indecency. In a later stage of my narrative I shall have to show that the "Liberal" Home Secretary has acted the part of an unscrupulous bigot, utterly regardless of truth, justice and honor.

I thought it my duty to write an open letter to Sir William Harcourt on the subject of his answer to Mr. Freshfield, in which I said—"I tell you that you could not suppress the Freethinker if you tried. The martyr spirit of Freethought is not dead, and the men who suffered imprisonment for liberty of speech a generation ago have not left degenerate successors. Should the necessity arise, there are Freethinkers who will not shrink from the same sacrifice for the same cause." The sequel has shown that this was no idle boast.

A few days later the Freethinker was again the subject of a question in the House. Mr. Redmond, member for New Ross, asked the Home Secretary "whether the Government had power to seize and summarily suppress newspapers which they considered pernicious to public morals; and, if so, why that power was not exercised in the case of the Freethinker and other papers now published and circulated in England." Sir William Harcourt repeated the answer he gave to Mr. Freshfield, and added that it would not be discreet to say whether the Government had power to seize obnoxious publications.

Mr. Redmond's question was a fine piece of impudence. Assuming that he represented all the voters in New Ross, his constituents numbered two hundred and sixty-one; and they could all be conveyed to Westminster in a tithe of the vehicles that brought people to Holloway Gaol to welcome me on the morning of my release. The total population of New Ross, including men, women and children, is less than seven thousand; a number that fell far short of the readers of the Freethinker even then. Representing a mere handful of people, Mr. Redmond had the audacity to ask for the summary suppression of a journal which is read in every part of the English-speaking world.

Nothing further of an exciting nature in connexion with my case occurred until early in May, when a prosecution for Blasphemy was instituted at Tunbridge Wells against Mr. Henry Seymour, Honorary Secretary of the local branch of the National Secular Society. This Branch had been the object of continued outrage and persecution, chiefly instigated, I have reason to believe, by Canon Hoare. The printed announcements outside their meeting-place were frequently painted over in presence of the police, who refused to interfere. Finally the police called on all the local bill-posters and warned them against exhibiting the Society's placards. Stung by these disgraceful tactics, Mr. Seymour issued a jocular programme of an evening's entertainment at the Society's hall, one profane sentence of which, while it in no way disturbed the peace or serenity of the town, aroused intense indignation in the breasts of the professional guardians of religion and morality. They therefore cited Mr. Seymour before the Justices of the Peace, and charged him with publishing a blasphemous libel. He was committed for trial at the next assizes, and in the meantime liberated on a hundred pounds bail. Acting under advice, Mr. Seymour pleaded guilty, and was discharged on finding sureties for his appearance when called up for judgment. This grievous error was a distinct encouragement to the bigots. Their appetite was whetted by this morsel, and they immediately sought a full repast.

My own attitude was one of defiance. In the Freethinker of May 14 I denounced the bigots as cowards for pouncing on a comparatively obscure member of the Freethought party, and I challenged them to attack its leaders before they assailed the rank and file. This challenge was cited against me on my own trial, but I do not regret it; and indeed I doubt if any man ever regretted that his sense of duty triumphed over his sense of danger.

CHAPTER II

OUR FIRST SUMMONS

Some day in the first week of July (I fancy it was Thursday, the 6th, but I cannot distinguish it with perfect precision, as some of my memoranda were scattered by my imprisonment) I enjoyed one of those very rare trips into the country which my engagements allowed. I was accompanied by two old friends, Mr. J. M. Wheeler and Mr. John Robertson, the latter being then on a brief first visit to London. We went up the river by boat, walked for hours about Kew and Richmond, and sat on the famous Terrace in the early evening, enjoying the lovely prospect, and discussing a long letter from Italy, written by one of our best friends, who was spending a year in that poet's paradise. How we chattered all through that golden day on all subjects, in the heavens above, on the earth beneath, and in the waters under the earth! With what fresh delight, in keeping with the scene, we compared our favorite authors and capped each other's quotations! Rare Walt Whitman told Mr. Conway that his forte was "loafing and writing poems." Well, we loafed too, and if we did not write poems, we startled the birds, the sheep, the cattle, and stray pedestrians, by reciting them. I returned home with that pleasant feeling of fatigue which is a good sign of health—with tired limbs and a clear brain, languid but not jaded. Throwing myself into the chair before my desk, I lit my pipe, and sat calmly puffing, while the incidents of that happy day floated through my memory as I watched the floating smoke-wreaths. Casually turning round, I noticed a queer-looking sheet of paper on the desk. I picked it up and read it. It was a summons from the Lord Mayor, commanding my attendance at the Mansion House on the following Tuesday, to answer a charge of Blasphemy. Strange ending to such a day! What a tragi-comedy life is—how full of contrasts and surprises, of laughter and tears.

Two others were summoned to appear with me: Mr. W. J. Ramsey, as publisher and proprietor, and Mr. E. W. Whittle, as printer. Mr. Bradlaugh, who was not included in the prosecution until a later stage of the proceedings, rendered us ungrudging assistance. Mr. Lickfold, of the well-known legal firm of Lewis and Lewis, was engaged to watch the case on behalf of Mr. Whittle. As for my own defence, I resolved from the very first to conduct it myself, a course for which I had excellent reasons, that were perfectly justified by subsequent events. In the Freethinker of July 30, 1882, I wrote:

> "I have to defend a principle as well as myself. The most skilful counsel might be half-hearted and over-prudent. Every lawyer looks to himself as well as to his client. When Erskine made his great speech at the end of last century in a famous trial for treason, Thomas Paine said it was a splendid speech for Mr. Erskine, but a very poor defence of the "Rights of Man." If Freethought is attacked it must be defended, and the charge of Blasphemy must be retorted on those who try to suppress liberty in the name of God. For my part, I would rather be convicted after my own defence than after another man's; and before I leave the court, for whatever destination, I will make the ears of bigotry tingle, and shame the hypocrites who profess and disbelieve."

For whatever destination! Yes, I avow that from the moment I read the summons I never had a doubt as to my fate. I knew that prosecutions for Blasphemy had invariably succeeded. How, indeed, could they possibly fail? I might by skill or luck get one jury to disagree, but acquittal was hopeless; and the prosecution could go on trying me until they found a jury sufficiently orthodox to ensure a verdict of guilty. It was a foregone conclusion. The prosecution played, "Heads I win, tails you lose."

And now a word as to our prosecutor. Nominally, of course, we were prosecuted by the Crown; and Judge North had the ignorance or impudence to tell the Old Bailey jury that this was not only theory but fact. Lord Coleridge, when he tried us two months later in the Court of Queen's Bench, told the jury that although the nominal prosecutor was the Crown, the actual prosecutor, the real plaintiff who set the Crown in motion, was Sir Henry Tyler. He provided all the necessary funds. Without his cash, nobody would have paid for the summons, and the pious lawyers, from Sir Hardinge Giffard downwards, who harangued the magistrates, the judge and the jury, would have held their venal tongues, and left poor Religion to defend herself as she could. And who is Sir Henry Tyler? or, rather, who was he? for after emerging into public notoriety by playing the part of a prosecutor, he fell back into his natural obscurity. He remained a Member of Parliament, but no one heard of him in that capacity, except now and then when he asked a foolish question, like others of his kind, who are mysteriously permitted to sit in our national legislature. Three years ago, however, he was a more conspicuous personage. He was then chairman of the Board of Directors of the Brush Light Company; and according to Henry Labouchere's statements in Truth, he was a "notorious guinea-pig." He was certainly an adept in the profitable transfer of shares: so much so, indeed, that at length the shareholders revolted against their pious chairman, and appointed a committee to investigate his proceedings. Whereupon this modern Knight of the Holy Ghost levanted, preferring to resign rather than face the inquiry. This is the man who asked in the House of Commons whether Mr. Bradlaugh's daughters could not be deprived of their hard-earned grants for their pupils who successfully passed the South Kensington examinations! This is the man who posed as the amateur champion of omnipotence! Surely if deity wanted a champion, Sir Henry Tyler is about the last person who would receive an application. Yet it is men of this stamp who have usually set the Blasphemy Laws in operation. These infamous laws are allowed to slumber for years, until some contemptible wretch, to gratify his private malice or a baser passion, rouses them into vicious activity, and fastens their fangs on men whose characters are far superior to his own. With this fact before them, it is strange that Christians should continue to regard these detestable laws as a bulwark of their faith, or in any way calculated to defend it against the inroads of "infidelity."

Sir Henry Tyler may after all have been a tool in the hands of others, for the St. Stephen's Review has admitted that the object of this prosecution was to cripple Mr. Bradlaugh in his parliamentary struggle, and we expected a prosecution long before it came, in consequence of some conversation on the subject overheard in the Tea Room of the House of Commons. But this, if true, while it heightens his insignificance, in no wise lessens his infamy; and it certainly does not impair, but rather increases, the force of my strictures on the Blasphemy Laws.

Lord Coleridge, in the Court of Queen's Bench, on the occasion of Mr. Bradlaugh's trial, sarcastically alluded to Sir Henry Tyler as "a person entirely unknown to me"—a very polite way of saying, "What does such an obscure person mean by assuming the role of Defender of the Faith?" His lordship must also have had that individual in his mind when, on the occasion of my own trial with Mr. Ramsey in the same Court on April 25, 1883, he delivered himself of these sentiments in the course of his famous summing-up:

"A difficult form of virtue is quietly and unostentatiously

to obey what you believe to be God's will in your own lives. It is not very easy to do that, and if you do it, you don't make much noise in the world. It is very easy to turn upon somebody who differs from you, and in the guise of zeal for God's honor, to attack somebody who differs from you in point of opinion, but whose life may be very much more pleasing to God, whom you profess to honor, than your own. When it is done by persons whose own lives are full of pretending to be better than their neighbors, and who take that particular form of zeal for God which consists in putting the criminal law in force against somebody else—that does not, in many people's minds, create a sympathy with the prosecutor, but rather with the defendant. There is no doubt that will be so; and if they should be men—I don't know anything about these persons—but if they should be men who enjoy the wit of Voltaire, and who do not turn away from the sneer of Gibbon, but rather relish the irony of Hume—one's feelings do not go quite with the prosecutor, but one's feelings are rather apt to sympathise with the defendants. It is still worse if the person who takes this course takes it not from a kind of rough notion that God wants his assistance, and that he can give it—less on his own account than by prosecuting other—or if it is mixed up with anything of a partisan or political nature. Then it is impossible that anything can be more foreign from one's notions of what is high-minded, religious and noble. Indeed, I must say it strikes me that anyone who would do that, not for the honor of God, but for his own purposes, is entitled to the most disdainful disapprobation that the human mind can form."

Some of the orthodox Tory journals censured Lord Coleridge for these scathing remarks, but his lordship is not easily frightened by anonymous critics, and it is probable that, if he ever has to try another case like ours, he may denounce the prosecutors in still stronger language if their motives are so obviously sinister as were those of Sir Henry Tyler.

There was a great crowd of people outside the Mansion House on Tuesday morning, May 11, and we were lustily cheered as we entered. Long before the Lord Mayor, Sir Whittaker Ellis, took his seat on the Bench, every inch of standing space in the Justice Room was occupied. Mr. Bradlaugh took a seat near Mr. Lickfold and frequently tendered us hints and advice. Mr. Ramsey, Mr. Whittle, and I took our places in the dock as our names were called out by Mr. Gresham, the chief clerk of the court. Our summons alleged that we unlawfully did publish, or caused to be published, certain blasphemous libels in a newspaper called the Freethinker, dated the 28th of May, 1882.

Mr. Maloney, who appeared for the prosecution, seemed fully impressed with the gravity of his position, and when he rose he had the air of a man who bore the responsibility of defending in his single person the honor, if not the very existence, of our national religion. His first proceeding was very characteristic of a gentleman with such a noble task. He attempted to hand in as evidence against us several numbers of the Freethinker not mentioned in the summons, and these would have been at once admitted by the Lord Mayor, who was apparently used to accepting evidence in an extremely free and easy fashion, as is generally the case with the "great unpaid"; but Mr. Lickfold promptly intervened, and his lordship, seeing the necessity of carefulness, then held that it would be advisable to adhere to the one case that morning, and to take out fresh summonses for the other numbers. Mr. Maloney then proceeded to deal with the numbers before the Court. There were numerous blasphemies which, if we were committed for trial, would be set forth in the indictment, but he would "spare the ears of the Court." One passage, however, he did read, and it is well to put on record, for the sake of those who talk about our "indecent" attacks on Christianity, what a prosecuting barrister felt he could rely on to procure our committal. It was as follows: "As for the Freethinker, he will scorn to degrade himself by going through the farce of reconciling his soul to a God whom he justly regards as the embodiment of crime and ferocity." Those words were not mine; they were from an article by one of my contributors; but I ask any reasonable man whether it is not ludicrous to prate about religious freedom in a country where writers run the risk of imprisonment for a sentence like that? As Mr. Maloney ended the quotation his voice sank to a supernatural whisper, he dropped the paper on the desk before him, and regarded his lordship with a look of pathetic horror, which the worthy magistrate fully reciprocated. As I contemplated these two voluntary augurs of our national faith, and at the same time remembered that far stronger expressions might be found in the writings of Mill, Clifford, Amberley, Arnold, Newman, Conway, Swinburne, and other works in Mudie's circulating library, I could scarcely refrain from laughter.

The witnesses for the prosecution were of the ordinary type—policemen, detectives, and lawyer's clerks—with the exception of Mr. Charles Albert Watts, who by accident or design found himself in such questionable company. This young gentleman is the son of Mr. Charles Watts and printer of the Secular Review, and he was called to prove that I was the editor of the Freethinker. With the most cheerful alacrity he positively affirmed that I was, although he had absolutely no more knowledge on the subject—as indeed he admitted on cross-examination—than any other member of the British public. His appearance in the witness-box is still half a mystery to me and I can only ask, Que le diable allait-il faire dans cette galere?

Ultimately the case was remanded till the following Monday, Mr. Maloney intimating that he should apply for fresh summonses for other numbers of the Freethinker, as well as a summons against Mr. Bradlaugh for complicity in our crime.

Let me here pause to consider how these prosecutions for blasphemy are initiated. Under the Newspaper Libels Act no prosecution for libel can be commenced against the editor, publisher or proprietor of any newspaper, without the written fiat of the Public Prosecutor. This post is occupied by Sir John Maule, who enjoys a salary of L2,000 a year, and has the assistance of a well-appointed office in his strenuous labors. Punch once pictured him fast asleep before the fire, with a handkerchief over his face, while all sorts of unprosecuted criminals plied their nefarious trades; and Mr. Justice Hawkins (I think) has denounced him as a pretentious farce. He is practically irresponsible, unlike the Attorney-General, who, being a member of the Government, is amenable to public opinion. Press laws, except in cases of personal libel, ought not to be neglected or enforced at the discretion of such an official. Every interference with freedom of speech, whenever it is deemed necessary, should be undertaken by the Government, or at least have its express sanction. Nothing of the sort happened in our case. On the contrary, Sir John Maule allowed our prosecution after Sir William Harcourt had condemned it. The Public Prosecutor set himself above the Home Secretary. Unfortunately the general press saw nothing anomalous or dangerous in such a state of things; for an official like Sir John Maule, while ready enough to sanction the prosecution of an unpopular journal, which presumably has few friends, is naturally reluctant, as events have shown, to allow proceedings against a powerful journal whose friends may be numerous and influential. Fortunately, however, a Select Committee of the House of Commons has taken a more sensible view of the Public Prosecutor and the duties he has so muddled, and recommended the abolition of his office. Should this step be taken, his duties will probably be performed by the Solicitor-General, and the press will be freed from a danger it had not the sense or the courage to avert. As for Sir John Maule, he will of course retire with a big pension, and live in fat ease for the rest of his sluggish life.

CHAPTER III

MR. BRADLAUGH INCLUDED

Mr. Maloney obtained his summons against Mr. Bradlaugh, whose name was included in a new document which was served on all of us. I have lost our first Summons, but I am able to give a copy of the second. It ran thus:

"TO WILLIAM JAMES RAMSEY, of 28 Stonecutter Street, in the City of London, and 20 Brownlow Street, Dalston, in the county of Middlesex; GEORGE WILLIAM FOOTE, of 9 South Crescent, Bedford Square, in the county of Middlesex; EDWARD WILLIAM WHITTLE, of 170 Saint John Street, Clerkenwell, in the county of Middlesex; and CHARLES BRADLAUGH, of 20 Circus Road, Saint John's Wood, in the county of Middlesex, and 28 Stonecutter Street, in the City of London.

"Whereas you have this day been charged before the under-signed, the Lord Mayor of the City of London, being one of Her Majesty's justices of the peace in and for the said City, and the liberties thereof, by Sir Henry Tyler, of Dashwood House, 9 New Broad Street, in the said City, for that you, in the said City, unlawfully did publish, or cause and procure to be published, certain blasphemous libels in a newspaper called the Freethinker, dated and published on the days following—that is to say, on the 26th day of March, 1882, on the 9th, 23rd and 30th days of April, 1882, and on the 7th, 14th, 21st and 28th days of May, 1882, and on the 11th and 18th days of June, 1882, against the peace, etc.:

"These are therefore to command you, in Her Majesty's name, to be and appear before me, on Monday, the 17th day of July, 1882, at eleven of the clock in the forenoon, at the Mansion House Justice-Room, in the said City, or before such other justice or justices of the peace for the same City as may then be there, to answer to the said charge, and to be further dealt with according to law. Herein fail not.

"Given under my hand and seal, this 12th day of July, in the year of our Lord 1882, at the Mansion House Justice-Room, aforesaid.
        "WHITTAKER ELLIS, Lord Mayor, London."

On the following Monday, July 17, the junior Member for

Northampton stood beside us in the Mansion House dock. The court was of course crowded, and a great number of people stood outside waiting for a chance of admission. The Lord Mayor considerately allowed us seats on hearing that the case would occupy a long time, a piece of attention which he might also have displayed on the previous Tuesday. It seems extremely unjust that men who are defending themselves, who need all their strength for the task, and who may after all be innocent, should be obliged to stand for hours in a crowded court in the dog-days, and waste half their energies in the perfectly gratuitous exertion of maintaining their physical equilibrium.

I shall not describe the proceedings before the Lord Mayor on this occasion. Properly speaking, it was Mr. Bradlaugh's day, and some time or other its incidents will be recorded in his biography. Suffice it to say that he showed his usual legal dexterity, sat on poor Mr. Maloney, and sadly puzzled the Lord Mayor. I must, however, refer to one point, as it illustrates the high Christian morality of our prosecutors. Mr. Maloney had obtained an illegal order from the Lord Mayor to inspect Mr. Bradlaugh's bank account, and armed with this order, which, even if it were legal, would not have extended beyond the limits of the City, this enterprising barrister had overhauled the books of the St. John's Wood Branch of the London and South-Western Bank. Lord Coleridge's astonishment at this unheard-of proceeding was only equalled by his trenchant sarcasm on the Lord Mayor as a legal functionary, and his bitter cold sneer at Mr. Maloney, who, it further appeared, had actually played the part of an amateur detective, by setting street policemen to watch Mr. Bradlaugh's entries and exits from his publishing office.

On the following Friday, July 21, the hearing of our case was resumed. We were all committed for trial at the Old Bailey, with the exception of Mr. Whittle, the printer, against whom the prosecution was abandoned on the ground that he had ceased to print the Freethinker. This was an unpleasant fact, and alas! it was only one of a good many I shall have to relate presently.

Before our committal I essayed to read a brief protest against the prosecution, which I had carefully prepared. In defiance of the statute, the Lord Mayor refused to hear it. An altercation then ensued, and I should have insisted on my right unless stopped by brute force; but on his lordship promising that a copy should be attached to the depositions, I yielded in order to let Mr. Bradlaugh have a full opportunity of stigmatising Sir Henry Tyler, who had left his questionable business at Dashwood House during a part of the day, to gloat over the spectacle of his enemy in a criminal dock.

Some portions of my half-suppressed protest ought not to be omitted in this history. After dealing in a few lines with the origin of the Blasphemy Laws, censuring the conduct of Sir Henry Tyler, and alluding to Sir. William Harcourt's reply to Mr. Freshfield, I expressed myself as follows:

"What, indeed, do the prosecutors hope or expect to gain? Freethought is no longer a weak, tentative, apologetic thing; it is strong, bold, and aggressive; and no law could now suppress it except one of extermination. Every breach made in its ranks by imprisonment would be instantly filled; and as punishment is not eternal on this side of death, the imprisoned man would some day return to his old place, fiercer than ever for the fight, and inflamed with an unappeasable hatred of the religion whose guardians prefer punishment to persuasion, and supplement the weakness of argument by the force of brutality.

"Blasphemy is a very general offence if we take even the lenient definitions of Sir James Stephen in his 'Digest of the Criminal Law.' All who publicly advocate the disestablishment of the Church are guilty under one clause, and half the leading writers of our age are guilty under another. It is difficult to find a book by any eminent scientist or thinker which does not contain open or covert attacks on Christianity and Scripture, and the Archbishop of Canterbury has pathetically complained that it is dangerous to introduce high-class magazines to the family circle, because they are nearly sure to contain a large quantity of scepticism. Why are these propagators of heresy never molested? Because it would be perilous to touch them. Prosecutions are always reserved for those who are unprotected by wealth and position. Heresy in expensive books for the upper classes is safe, but heresy in cheap publications for the people incurs a terrible danger. The one is flattered and conciliated, while the other is liable at any moment to be put on its defence in a criminal court, and is always at the mercy of any man who may choose to indulge his political animosity, his social enmity, or his private spite.

"Blasphemy is entirely a matter of opinion. What is blasphemy in one country is piety in another. Progress tends to reduce it from a crime to an affair of taste. To deal with it in the bad spirit of the old laws, which are only unrepealed because they have been treated as obsolete, is to outrage the conscience of civilisation, and to violate that liberty of the press which Bentham justly called 'the foundation of all other liberties.' If opinions are not forced on people's attention, if they are expressed in publications which are sold, which can be patronised

or neglected, and which must be deliberately sought before they can be read; then, unless they contain incitements to crime, they are entitled to immunity from molestation, and to interfere with them is the height of gratuitous impertinence."

In the ordinary course our Indictment would have been tried at the Old Bailey. The grand jury found a true bill against us, after being charged by the Recorder, Sir Thomas Chambers, who addressed them as fellow Christians, quite forgetful of the fact that Jews and Deists are eligible as jurymen no less than orthodox believers. According to the newspapers this bigot described our blasphemous libels as "shocking," and said that "it was impossible for any Christian man to read them without feeling that they came within that description, and they ought to return a true bill." This same Sir Thomas Chambers is a patron of piety, especially when it takes the form of aggressive polemics. Some time afterwards he joined a committee, with the late Lord Shaftesbury, Lord Mayor Fowler, and other religious worthies, whose object was to raise a testimonial to Samuel Kinns, an obscure author who has written a stupid volume on "Moses and Geology" for the purpose of showing that the book of Genesis, to use Huxley's expression, contains the beginning and the end of sound science. It thus appears that a Christian magistrate may subscribe (or, which is quite as pious and far more economical, induce others to subscribe) for the confutation of heretics, and afterwards send them to gaol for not being confuted. What a glorious commentary on the great truth that England is a free country, and that Christianity relies entirely on the force of persuasion! Fortunately, however, our case was not tried at the Old Bailey. Mr. Bradlaugh obtained a writ of certiorari removing the indictment to the Court of Queen's Bench, where our case was put in the Crown List, and did not come on for hearing until two months after I was imprisoned on another indictment. Mr. Bradlaugh obtained the writ on July 29, 1882. It was during the long vacation, and we had to appear before more than one judge in chambers, Mr. Justice Stephen being the one who granted the writ. I remember roaming the Law Courts with Mr. Bradlaugh that morning. We went from office to office in the most perplexing manner. Everything seemed designed to baffle suitors who conduct their own cases. Obsolete technicalities, only half intelligible even to experts, met one at every turn, and when I left the Law Courts I felt that the thing was indeed done, but that it would almost puzzle omniscience to do it again in exactly the same way. Over seven pounds was spent in stamps, documents, and other items; and I was informed that a solicitor's charges for the morning's work would have exceeded thirty pounds. Securities for costs were required to the extent of six hundred pounds, and of course they had to be given. Yet we were merely seeking justice and a fair trial! As I walked home I pondered the great truth that England is a free country, and that there is one law for the rich and the poor; yet I reflected that as only the rich could afford it, the poor might as well have no law at all.

I have already referred to our printer's defection. Acting under advice, Mr. Whittle declined to print the Comic Bible Sketch in the number for July 16, and the following week he refused to print at all. He announced this decision after all the type was set up and the "formes" were almost ready for the press. Only forty-eight hours remained before the Freethinker was due. During that period, in company with my friend and sub-editor, Mr. J. M. Wheeler, I made desperate efforts to get a printer to undertake the work. At last I discovered a Freethinker who placed his inadequate resources at my disposal. He could only set up four pages of type, and only print copies with a hand-press. Even that was better than nothing; anything being preferable to lowering the flag in the heat of battle. But alas! fate is stronger than gods or men. I was foiled at the last moment, just as victory seemed within my grasp; how I forbear to explain, although the incidents of that eventful day would form an interesting chapter of my Autobiography. Enough copies were pulled to constitute a legal issue of the paper, and one of these is safely deposited in the British Museum; but none were printed for the market, and it was everywhere reported that the Freethinker was dead. Christian Evidence lecturers joyously announced the fact at their meetings, and Mr. Maloney ironically alluded to it in Court. I bore all these taunts with grim silence, which was at last broken, not by words, but by deeds. These people did not know that the Freethinker, like the founder of their faith, had disappeared one week only to reappear the next. With the aid of Mr. Ramsey, who again stood by our side, we succeeded in restoring our paper to the light of day. Type was purchased, compositors were engaged, and a little shop was taken in Harp Alley. The Freethinker for July 30 struck astonishment into the souls of those who had rejoiced over its death when they saw no Freethinker for July 23. From that moment our issue was never once suspended, although we had some desperate close shaves.

In the number for August 6, as I could not get our machiner to print any Comic Bible Sketches just then, I published a serious one, reproduced from an old Dutch Bible of 1669. It represented Moses obtaining a panoramic view of Jehovah's back parts. Below the text I inserted the following notice: "As the bigots object to our Comic

Bible Sketches, we shall publish a few Serious Bible Sketches, copied accurately from old Bibles of the ages of faith, to show what the Christians have done themselves in the way of familiar interpretation. We hope the bigots will like the change." By the next week, however, I had overcome our machiner's scruples, and the Comic Bible Sketches were resumed and continued up to the day of my imprisonment.

My attitude towards the prosecution is amply expressed by these facts, but a few words from my pen at that time may not be altogether superfluous. In an article entitled "Crucify Him!" in the Freethinker of August 6, 1882, I wrote:

"We are charged with blasphemy, and so was Jesus Christ. What a grim joke it will be if the Freethinker is found guilty and punished for the same crime as the preacher of the Sermon on the Mount! Truly adversity makes us acquainted with strange bedfellows.

"Yet, whatever happens, we will not quail. We will not vapor about legions of angels, but trust in the living legions of Freethought. We will not yield to the weakness of an agony and bloody sweat, nor pray that the cup may pass from us, nor cry out that we are forsaken; for our sources of strength are all within us, and cannot be taken away. We have a sense of truth, a conviction of right, and a spirit of courage, caught from the gallant men who fought before. Let the bigots do their worst; they will not break our spirit nor extinguish our cause. Let the Christian mob clamor as loudly as they can, 'Crucify him, crucify him!' They will not daunt us. We look with prophetic eyes over all the tumult, and see in the distance the radiant form of Liberty, bearing in her left hand the olive branch and in her right hand the sword, the holy victress, destined by treaty or conquest to bring the whole world under her sway. And across all the din we hear her great rich voice, banishing despair, inspiring hope, and infusing a joyous ardour in every nerve."

From the first I was sure that the Freethought party would support those who were fighting its battle, and I was not deceived. The Freethinker Defence Fund was liberally subscribed to throughout the country, several working men putting by a few pence every week for the purpose; and as I travelled up and down on my lecturing tours I experienced everywhere the heartiest greetings. I saw that the party's blood was up, and that however it might ultimately fare with me, the battle would be fought to the bitter end.

Considerable controversy took place in the daily and weekly press. Professor W. A. Hunter contributed a timely letter to the Daily News, in which he described the Blasphemy Laws as "a weapon always ready to the hand of mischievous fools or designing knaves." Mr. G. J. Holyoake wrote in his usual vein of covert attack on Freethinkers in danger. Mrs. Besant joined in the fray anonymously, and a letter appeared also from my own pen. There were articles on the subject in the provincial newspapers, and amongst the London journals I must especially commend the Weekly Dispatch, which never wavered in faithfulness to its Liberal traditions, and stood firm in its censure of our prosecution from first to last, even when other journals turned from the path of religious liberty, proved traitors to their principles, and joined the bigots in their cry of "To prison, to prison!" against the obnoxious heretics.

For some time after this we pursued the even tenor of our way. Many of the wholesale newsagents, who had been frightened when our prosecution was initiated, regained confidence and resumed their orders. Early in October we removed from Harp Alley to 28 Stonecutter Street, which had just been vacated by the Freethought Publishing Company, and which has ever since been the publishing office of the Freethinker. About the same time I issued a pamphlet entitled "Blasphemy no Crime," a copy of which was sent to every newspaper in the United Kingdom. It traversed the whole field of discussion, and gave a brief history of past prosecutions for Blasphemy, as well as the principal facts of our own case. In November I announced the preparation of the second Christmas Number of the Freethinker, the publication for which I paid the penalty of twelve months' imprisonment. Before, however, I deal fully with that awful subject I will redeem my promise to inform my readers of the nature of our indictment, and what were the actual charges preferred against us by Sir Henry Tyler on behalf of the insulted universe.

CHAPTER IV

OUR INDICTMENT

Our Indictment covered twenty-eight large folios, and contained sixteen Counts. Of course we had to pay for a copy of it; for although a criminal is supposed to enjoy the utmost fair play, and according to legal theory is entitled to every advantage in his defence, as a matter of fact, unless he is able to afford the cost of a copy, he has no right to know the contents of his Indictment until he stands in the dock to plead to it.

It was evidently drawn up by someone grossly ignorant of the Bible. The Apocalypse was described as the "Book of Revelations," and the Gadarean swine came out as Gadderean. Probably Sir Henry Tyler and Sir Hardinge Giffard knew as much of the Scriptures they strove to imprison us for disputing as the person who drew up our Indictment. Mr. Cluer caused some amusement in the Court of Queen's Bench when, in the gravest manner, he drew attention to these errors. Lord Coleridge as gravely replied that he could not take judicial cognisance of them. Whereupon Mr. Cluer quietly observed that he was ready to produce the authorised version of the Bible in court in a few minutes, as he had a copy in his chambers. This remark elicited a smile from Lord Coleridge, a broad grin from the lawyers in Court, and a titter from the crowd. It was perfectly understood that a gentleman of the long robe might prosecute anybody for blasphemy against the Bible and its Deity, but the idea of a barrister having a copy of the "sacred volume" in his chambers was really too absurd for belief.

The preamble charged us, in the stock language of Indictments for Blasphemy, as may be seen on reference to Archibold, with "being wicked and evil-disposed persons, and disregarding the laws and religion of the realm, and wickedly and profanely devising and intending to asperse and vilify Almighty God, and to bring the Holy Scriptures and the Christian Religion into disbelief and contempt."

The first observation I have to make on this wordy jumble is, that it seems highly presumptuous on the part of weak men to defend the character of "Almighty God." Surely they might leave him to protect himself. Omnipotence is able to punish those who offend it, and Omniscience knows when to punish. Man's interference is grossly impertinent. When the emperor Tiberius was asked by an informer to allow proceedings against one who had "blasphemed the gods," he replied: "No, let the gods defend their own honor." Christian rulers have not yet reached that level of justice and common sense.

Next, it was flagrantly unjust to accuse us of aspersing and vilifying Almighty God at all. The Freethinker had simply assailed the reputation of the god of the Bible, a tribal deity of the Jews, subsequently adopted by the Christians, whom James Mill had described as "the most perfect conception of wickedness which the human mind can devise." What difference, I ask, is there between that strong description and the sentence quoted from the Freethinker in our Indictment, which declared the same being as "cruel as a Bashi-Bazouk and bloodthirsty as a Bengal tiger"? The one is an abstract and the other a concrete expression of the same view; the one is philosophical and the other popular; the one is a cold statement and the other a burning metaphor. To allow the one to circulate with impunity, and to punish the other with twelve months' imprisonment, is to turn a literary difference into a criminal offence.

Further, as Sir James Stephen has observed, it is absurd to talk about bringing "the Holy Scriptures and the Christian religion into disbelief and contempt." One of these words is clearly superfluous. Considering the extraordinary pretensions of the Bible and Christianity, it is difficult to see how they could be brought into contempt more effectually than by bringing them into disbelief.

But greater absurdities remain. Our Indictment averred that we had published certain Blasphemous Libels "to the great displeasure of Almighty God, to the scandal of the Christian religion and the Holy Bible or Scriptures, and against the peace of our Lady the Queen, her crown and dignity." Let us analyse this legal jargon.

How did our prosecutors learn that we displeased Almighty God? In what manner did Sir Henry Tyler first become aware of the fact? Was it, in the ancient fashion, revealed to him in a dream, or did it come by direct inspiration? What was the exact language of the aggrieved Deity? Did he give Sir Henry Tyler a power of attorney to defend his character by instituting a prosecution for libel? If so, where is the document, and who will prove the signature? And did the original party to the suit intimate his readiness to be subpoenaed as a witness at the trial? All these are very important questions, but there is no likelihood of their ever being answered.

"The scandal of the Christian Religion" is an impertinent joke. Christianity, as Lord Coleridge remarked, is no longer, as the old judges used to rule, part and parcel of the law of England. I argued the matter at considerable length in addressing the jury, and his lordship supported my contention with all the force of his high authority. After pointing out that at one time Jews, Roman Catholics, and Nonconformists of all sorts—in fact every sect outside the State Church—were under heavy disabilities for religion and regarded as hardly having civil rights, and that undoubtedly at that time the doctrines of the Established religion were part and parcel of the law of the land, Lord Coleridge observed, as I had done, that "Parliament, which is supreme and binds us all, has enacted statutes which make that view of the law no longer applicable." I had also pointed out that there might be a Jew on the jury. His lordship went further, and remarked that there might be a Jew on the bench. His words were these:

> "Now, so far as I know, a Jew might be Lord Chancellor; most certainly he might be Master of the Rolls. The great and illustrious lawyer [Sir George Jessel] whose loss the whole profession is deploring, and in whom his friends know that they lost a warm friend and a loyal colleague; he, but for the accident of taking his office before the Judicature Act came into operation, might have had to go circuit, might have sat in a criminal court to try such a case as this, might have been called upon, if the law really be that 'Christianity is part of the law of the land' in the sense contended for, to lay it down as law to a jury, amongst whom might have been Jews,—that it was an offence against the law, as blasphemy, to deny that Jesus Christ was the Messiah, a thing which he himself did deny, which Parliament had allowed him to deny, and which it is just as much part of the law that anyone may deny, as it is your right and mine, if we believe it, to assert."

Clearly then, according to the dictum of the Lord Chief Justice, it is not a crime to publish anything "to the scandal of the Christian Religion," although it was alleged against us as such in our Indictment.

The only real point that can be discussed and tested is in the last clause. I do not refer to the Queen's "crown and dignity," which we were accused of endangering; for our offence could not possibly be construed as a political one, and it is hard to perceive how the Queen's dignity could be imperilled by the act of any person except herself. What I refer to is the statement that we had provoked a disturbance of the peace; a more hypocritical pretence than which was never advanced. I venture to quote here a passage from my address to the jury on my third trial before Lord Coleridge:—

> "A word, gentlemen, about breach of the peace. Mr. Justice Stephen said well, that no temporal punishment should be inflicted

for blasphemy unless it led to a breach of the peace. I have no objection to that, provided we are indicted for a breach of the peace. Very little breach of the peace might make a good case of blasphemy. A breach of the peace in a case like this must not be constructive; it must be actual. They might have put somebody in the witness-box who would have said that reading the Freethinker had impaired his digestion and disturbed his sleep. They might have even found somebody who said it was thrust upon him, and that, he was induced to read it, not knowing its character. Gentlemen, they have not attempted to prove that any special publicity was given to it outside the circle of the people who approved it. They have not even shown there was an advertisement of it in any Christian or religious paper. They have not even told you that any extravagant display was made of it; and I undertake to say that you might never have known of it if the prosecution had not advertised it. How can all this be construed as a breach of the peace? Our Indictment says we have done all this, to the great displeasure of Almighty God, and to the danger of our Lady the Queen, her crown and dignity. You must bear that in mind. The law-books say again and again that a blasphemous libel is punished, not because it throws obloquy on the deity—the protection of whom would be absurd— but because it tends to a breach of the peace. It is preposterous to say such a thing tends to a breach of the peace. If you want that you must go to the Salvation Army. They have a perfect right to their ideas—I have nothing to say about them; but their policy has led to actual breaches of the peace; and even in India, where, according to the law, no prosecution could be started against a paper like the Freethinker, many are sent to gaol because they will insist upon processions in the street. We have not caused tumult in the streets. We have not sent out men with banners and bands in which each musician plays more or less his own tune. We have not sent out men who make hideous discord, and commit a common nuisance. Nothing of the sort is alleged. A paper like this had to be bought and our utterances had to be sought. We have not done anything against the peace. I give the Indictment an absolute denial. To talk of danger to the peace is only a mask to hide the hideous and repulsive features of intolerance and persecution. They don't want to punish us because we have assailed religion, but because we have endangered the peace. Take them at their word, gentlemen. Punish us if we have endangered the peace, and not if we have assailed religion; and as you know we have not endangered the peace, you will of course bring in a verdict of Not Guilty. Gentlemen, I hope you will by your verdict to-day champion that great law of liberty which is challenged—the law of liberty which implies the equal right of everyman, while he

> does not trench upon the equal right of every other man, to print what he pleases for people who choose to buy and read it, so long as he does not libel men's characters or incite people to the commission of crime."

Appealing now to a far larger jury in the high court of public opinion, I ask whether Freethinkers are not one of the most orderly sections of the community. Why should we resort to violence, or invoke it, or even countenance it, when our cardinal principle is the sovereignty of reason, and our hope of progress lies in the free play of mind on every subject? We are perhaps more profoundly impressed than others with the idea that all institutions are the outward expression of inward thoughts and feelings, and that it is impossible to forestall the advance of public sentiment by the most cunningly-devised machinery. We are par excellence the party of order, though not of stagnation. It is a striking and pregnant fact that Freethought meetings are kept peaceful and orderly without any protection by the police. At St. James's Hall, London, the only demonstrations, I believe, for which the services of a certain number of policemen are not charged for in the bill with the rent, are those convened by Mr. Bradlaugh and his friends.

Lord Coleridge, ostensibly but not actually following Michaelis, raised the subtle argument that as people's feelings are very tender on the subject of religion, and the populace is apt to take the law into its own hands when there is no legal method of expressing its anger and indignation, "some sort of blasphemy laws reasonably enforced may be an advantage even to those who differ from the popular religion of a country, and who desire to oppose and to deny it." But this is an inversion of the natural order of things. What reason is there in imprisoning an innocent man because some one meditates an assault upon him? Would it not be wiser and juster to restrain the intending criminal, as is ordinarily done? I object to being punished because others cannot keep their tempers; and I say further, that to punish a man, not because he has injured others, but for his own good, is the worst form of persecution. During the many years of my public advocacy of Freethought in all parts of Great Britain, both before and since my imprisonment, I have never been in a moment's danger of violence and outrage. I never witnessed any irritation which could not be allayed by a persuasive word, or any disturbance that could not be quelled by a witticism. With all deference to Lord Coleridge, whom no one admires and respects more than I do, I would rather the law left me to my own resources, and only interfered to protect me when I need its assistance.

Now for the counts of our Indictment. There is danger in writing about them, as it is held that the publication of matter found blasphemous by a jury, except in a legal report for the profession, is itself blasphemy, and may be punished as such. I am not, however, likely to be deterred from my purpose by this consideration. On the other hand, as the incriminated passages were all carefully selected from many numbers of a journal never remarkable for its tender treatment of orthodoxy, I do not see any particular advantage to be derived from their republication. They are, of course, far more calculated to shock religious susceptibilities (if these are to be considered) when they are picked out and ranked together than when they stand amid their context in their original places. Such a process of selection would be exceedingly hard on any paper or book handling very advanced ideas, and very backward ones, in a spirit of great freedom. Nay, it would prove a severe trial to most works of real value, whose scope extended beyond the respectabilities. Not to mention Byron's caustic remarks on the peculiar expurgation of Martial in Don Juan's edition, it is obvious that the Bible and Shakespeare could both be proved obscene by this process; and setting aside ancient literature altogether, half our own classics, before the age of Wordsworth and Scott, would come under the same condemnation. I know I am intruding among my betters; but I do not claim equality with them; I merely ask the same liberal judgment. A man is no more to be judged by a few casual sentences from his pen, without any reference to all the rest, than he is to be judged by a few casual expressions he may let fall in a year's conversation.

Curiously, in all those twenty-eight folios of blasphemy, only three sentences were from my own pen, and two of them were extracted from long articles. One was a jocose reference to the Jewish tribal god, who, as Keunen allows, was carried about, probably as a stone fetish, in that wooden box known as the "ark of the covenant." Another occurred in a long review of Jules Soury's remarkable book on the subject of Jesus Christ's hallucinations and eccentricities, in which he endeavors to show that the Prophet of Nazareth passed through certain recognised stages of brain disease. Referring to the close of his career, I wrote that, "When Jesus made his triumphant entry into Jerusalem he was plainly crazed." That one sentence was picked out from a long review, running through three numbers of the Freethinker, and filling six columns of print. The third sentence was a satirical comment on the sensational and blasphemous title of Dr. Parker's book on "The Inner Life of Christ." I asked, "How did he contrive to get inside his maker?" There was a fourth sentence I wrote for the Freethinker, but as it was a verbatim report of some Bedlamite observations of a Salvationist at Halifax, published, as I said, "to show what is being done and said in the name of Christianity," I decline to be held responsible for it. Let General Booth be answerable for the blasphemies of his own followers.

All the other passages in the Indictment were from the pens of contributors, over whom, as they signed their articles, I never held a tight rein. They were mostly amplifications of the sentence I have already quoted about the cruel character of the Bible God. I did not, however, dwell on this fact in my address to the jury. I took the full responsibility, and fought my contributors' battle as well my own. I bore their iniquities, the chastisement of their peace was upon me, and by my stripes they were healed.

Four of the Comic Bible Sketches were included in the Indictment. They appeared in the Freethinker on the following dates:—January 29, April 23, May 28, and June 11 (1882). Readers who care to see what they were like can refer to the file in the British Museum. Those illustrations have not been declared blasphemous, for when the Indictment I have been explaining was tried before Lord Coleridge, the jury, after several hours' deliberation, could not agree to a verdict of Guilty.

The Indictment on which I was found guilty, and sentenced to twelve months' imprisonment, was a later one. It was based on the Christmas Number, 1882, to which I previously referred. Let me now give a brief history of my second prosecution.

CHAPTER V

ANOTHER PROSECUTION

In the month of November (1882) I announced my intention to bring out a new monthly magazine entitled Progress. Several friends thought it impolitic to launch my new venture in such troubled waters, and advised me to wait for the issue of the prosecution. But I resolved to act exactly as though the prosecution had never been initiated. It seemed to me the wisest course to go on with my work until I was stopped, and risk the consequences whatever they might be. The result has proved that I was right; but I do not wish to boast of my judgment, for when I was imprisoned all my interests were fearfully imperilled, and everything depended on the loyal exertions of a few staunch Freethinkers (of whom more anon) who stepped into the breach and defended them with great courage and ability until I was able to resume my post. Progress made its due appearance in January, 1883, and, notwithstanding the extraordinary vicissitudes of its career, it has flourished ever since without any solution of continuity.

While I was advertising Progress I was also preparing the second Christmas Number of the Freethinker. The announcement of its contents caused a great deal of excitement, and I am prepared to admit that it was, to use a common phrase, the "warmest" publication ever issued. It was full from cover to cover of what the orthodox call blasphemy, and it was speedily described by the Christian press as more "outrageous" than any of the ordinary numbers for which we were already prosecuted. The description was perfectly correct. I had concluded that my wisest policy, as it was certainly the most courageous, was to disregard the Blasphemy Laws and defy the bigots; to show that Freethought was not to be cowed or intimidated by threats of imprisonment. Facing the enemy boldly appeared to me better than running away; a course in which I could see neither glory, honor, nor profit. Even if I had consulted my safety above all things, I should have seen little wisdom in flight; and being shot in the back, while no less dangerous, is far more ignominious than being shot in the front. I have paid the full penalty of my policy; I have suffered twelve months' torture in a Christian gaol; yet I do not repent the course I took; and ever since my release from prison I have felt it my duty to continue doing the very thing for which I was punished.

Being tastefully got-up, well printed, profusely illustrated, and extensively denounced by the organs of Toryism and piety, this Christmas Number had a very large sale. Yet, strange as it may sound to some bigoted ears, Mr. Ramsey and I were after all several pounds out of pocket by it, the expenses being altogether out of proportion to the price, and our object being less material gain than the wide dissemination of our views. With the knowledge of this pecuniary loss in our minds, it may be imagined how grimly we smiled when the counsel sternly alluded to our "nefarious profits."

I shall have occasion to deal with the contents of this Christmas Number when I explain our second Indictment; which, I repeat, as there is general misunderstanding on the subject, was tried before the first, and resulted in Judge North's atrocious and almost unparalleled sentence.

During the interval between the publication of this "budget of blasphemy" and the date of our summons to answer a criminal charge founded on it, I had several interviews with Mr. E. Truelove, a gentleman well known to all advanced people in London as a veteran champion of the freedom as the press. At the age of seventy, after a long life sans peur et sans reproche, this fine old reformer was dragged by the paid Secretary of the Society for the Suppression of Vice (or the Vice Society as Cobbett always called it) into a criminal court to answer a charge of obscenity. The objectionable matter was contained in an extremely mild, not to say mawkish, essay on the population question by Robert Dale Owen, a man of literary eminence in the United States, and once an ambassador of the great Republic. Like ourselves, Mr. Truelove was tried twice before a verdict of guilty could be obtained. His sentence was four months' imprisonment like a common felon. Mr. Truelove was indisposed to reveal the secrets of his prison-house out of a tender regard for my feelings, but seeing that I preferred to know the worst, he told me all about the felon's cell, the plank bed, the oakum picking, the wretched diet, and the horribly monotonous life. My chief feeling on hearing this sad tale was one of indignation at the thought that a man of honest convictions and blameless life should be subjected to such privations and indignities. It did not weaken my resolution; it only deepened my hatred of the system which sanctioned such iniquities.

From America, however, came a piece of bitter-sweet news. Mr. D. M. Bennett, editor of the New York Truthseeker, had just died. His end was hastened by the heart-disease he contracted while undergoing imprisonment for an "offence" similar to that of Mr. Truelove. Yet almost at the moment of Mr. Bennett's death, another jury had found another publisher of the very same work Not Guilty. I learned from the New York papers that the acquittal was partly due to the impartiality of the judge, partly to the progress the public mind had made on the population question, and partly to the fact that the accused publisher conducted his own defence. Here was a gleam of hope. I also might meet with an impartial judge, I also might find a jury reflecting an enlightened public opinion, and I also was resolved to defend myself. Alas! I did not know that I was to meet with the most bigoted judge on the bench, and to plead to a jury exactly calculated to effect his vindictive purpose.

On Thursday, December 7, 1882, we published our second Christmas Number of the Freethinker. I will deal with its contents presently, when I have narrated how it led to our second prosecution. Let it here suffice to say that it was undoubtedly a very "warm" publication, and well calculated to arouse the slumbering Blasphemy Laws. Some Freethinkers even were astonished at its audacity. A few belonging to an old-fashioned school, and a few more who were assiduously courting "respectability," resented our action; although, as the vast majority of our party were of an opposite opinion, they refrained from expressing their reprobation too loudly. In reply to their murmurs I wrote an article in my paper on "Superstitious Freethinkers." It appeared in the number for December 31, and thus appropriately closed a year of combat. A few passages are, perhaps, worth insertion here.

"It has been said of Robert Burns that, although his head and heart rejected Calvinism, he never quite got it out of his blood. There is much truth in this metaphor. Burns was, in religious matters, one of a very large class. Many men rid their intellects of a superstition, without being able to resist its power over their feelings. Even so profound a sceptic as Renan has admitted that his life is guided by a faith he no longer possesses. And we are all familiar with instances of the same thing..."

"Reverting to avowed Freethinkers, it is evident that some of them who have lost belief in God are afraid to speak too loud lest he should overhear them. 'How old are you, Monsieur Fontenelle?' asked a pretty young French lady. 'Hush, not so loud, dear Madame!' replied the witty nonagenarian, pointing upwards. What Fontenelle did as a piece of graceful wit, some Freethinkers do without any wit at all. They object to laughing at the gods, whether Christian, Brahmanic or Mohammedan; and perhaps they would extend the same friendly consideration to Mumbo Jumbo. Strange that people should be so tender about ghosts! Especially when they don't even believe them to be

real ghosts. To the Atheist all gods are fancies, mere delusions (not illusions), like the philosopher's stone, witchcraft, astrology, holy water and miracles. I am as much entitled to ridicule the gods of Christianity as any other Freethinker is entitled to ridicule the miracles at Lourdes; and when 'taste' is dragged into the question, I simply reply that there is as much ill taste in the one case as in the other. All that this 'taste' can mean is that no devout delusion should be ridiculed, which is itself one of the greatest pieces of absurdity ever perpetrated. It would shield every form of 'spiritual' lunacy in the world.

"These squeamish Freethinkers don't object to ridicule in politics, literature or social life. They rather approve Punch and the other comic journals, even when these satirise living persons who feel the sting. Why, then, do they object to ridicule in religion? Simply because they still feel that there is something sacred about it. Now I insist that on the Atheist's principles there can be no such sacredness, and I decline to recognise it. I take the full consequences and claim the full liberty of my belief.

"Christians may, of course, urge that their feelings on such a subject as religion are sacred, and a few superstitious Freethinkers may concede this monstrous position. I do not. The feelings of a Christian about Father, Son and Holy Ghost, are no more sacred than my feelings on any other subject. I have no quarrel with persons, and I recognise how many are hurt by satire. But the world is not to be regulated by their feelings, and much as I respect them, I have a greater respect for truth. Every mental weapon is valid against mental error. And as ridicule has been found the most potent weapon of religious enfranchisement, we are bound to use it against the wretched superstitions which cumber the path of progress. Intellectually, it is as absurd to give quarter as it is absurd to expect it.

"My answer to the Freethinkers who would coquet with Christianity, and gain a fictitious respectability by courting compliments from Christian teachers, is that they are playing with fire. Let them ponder the lessons of history, and remember Clifford's bitter word about the evil superstition which destroyed one civilisation and nearly succeeded in destroying another. Fortunately, however, the logic of things is against them. Broad currents of thought go on their way without being deflected by backwashes, or eddies or spurts into blind passages. Freethought will sweep on with its main volume, and dash against every impediment with all its effective force."

Well, I exercised "the full liberty of my belief," and I had to take its "full consequences." Yet, looking back over my year's torture in a Christian gaol, my conscience approves that dangerous policy, and I do not experience a single regret.

In the same number of the Freethinker I referred at some length to Tyler's prosecution, which was dragging along its slow course in a way that must have been very provoking to Mr. Bradlaugh's enemies. By dexterous manoeuvring and skilful pleading, that litigious man, as the Tories call him, had managed to get two counts struck out of our Indictment. The result of this to Mr. Ramsey and myself was nil, but it brought great relief to Mr. Bradlaugh, and made his acquittal almost a matter of certainty.

Meanwhile our Christmas Number was selling rapidly. In a few weeks it had reached a far larger circulation than had been enjoyed by any Freethought publication before. Naturally the bigots were enraged, both by its character and its success. Many religious journals, and especially the Rock, clamored for legal protection against such "blasphemy." Irate Christians called at our shop in Stonecutter Street, purchased copies of the obnoxious paper, and, flourishing them in the faces of Mr. Ramsey and Mr. Kemp, declared that we should "hear more of this;" to which pious salutation they usually replied by offering their minatory visitors "a dozen or perhaps a quire at trade price." Similar busybodies called at Mr. Cattell's shop in Fleet Street, and plied him with cajoleries when menaces were futile. One of them, indeed, attempted bribery. He offered Mr. Cattell half a sovereign to remove our Christmas Number from his window. What a wonderful bigot! That detestable fraternity has nearly always persecuted heresy at other people's expense, but this man was willing to tax himself for that laudable object. Surely he is phenomenal enough to deserve a memorial in Westminster Abbey, or at least an effigy at Madame Tussaud's.

Presently our shop was visited by another class of men—plainclothes detectives. They came in couples, and it was easy to understand their business. We were, therefore, not surprised when, on January 29, 1883, we were severally served with the following summons:—

"To GEORGE WILLIAM FOOTE, of No. 9 South Crescent, Bedford Square,
 Middlesex; WILLIAM JAMES RAMSEY, of No. 28 Stonecutter Street, in the City of London, and No. 20 Brownlow Street, Dalston,
 Middlesex; and HENRY ARTHUR KEMP, of No. 28 Stonecutter Street, aforesaid, and No. 15 Harp Alley, Farringdon Street, London, E.C.

Whereas you have this day been charged before the undersigned, the Lord Mayor of the City of London, being one of her Majesty's Justices of the Peace in and for the said City and the Liberties thereof, by JAMES MACDONALD, of No. 7 Burton Road, Brixton, in the county of Surrey, for that you did in the said City of London, on the 16th day December, in the year of Our Lord, 1882, and on divers other days, print and publish, and cause and procure to be printed and published, a certain blasphemous and impious libel in the Christmas Number for 1882 of a certain newspaper called the Freethinker, against the peace of our Lady the Queen, her crown and Dignity. These are therefore to command you, in her Majesty's name, to be and appear before me on Friday, the second day of February, 1883, at eleven of the clock in the forenoon, at the Mansion House Justice Room, in the said City, or before such other Justice or Justices of the Peace for the same City as may then be there, to answer to the said charge, and to be further dealt with according to law. Herein fail not. Given under my hand and seal, this 29th day of January, in the year of Our Lord, 1883, at the Mansion House Justice-Room aforesaid.

"HENRY E. KNIGHT,
"Lord Mayor, London."

The James Macdonald of this summons, who played the part of a common informer, turned out to be a police officer. In the ordinary way of business he went to the Lord Mayor, complained of our blasphemy and his own lacerated feelings, and applied for a summons against us as a first step towards punishing us for our sins. What a reductio ad absurdum of the Blasphemy Laws! Instead of ordinary Christians protesting against our outrages, and demanding our restraint in the interest of the peace, a callous policeman has to do the work, without a scintilla of feeling about the matter, just as he might proceed against any ordinary criminal for theft or assault. The real mover in this business was Sir Thomas Nelson, the City Solicitor, representing the richest and corruptest Corporation in the world.

The Corporation of the City of London might be described in the language which Jesus applied to the Town Council of Jerusalem eighteen centuries ago—"They devour widows' houses, and for a pretence make long prayers." What could be more hypocritical than such a body posing as the champions of religion, and especially of the religion of Christ! If the Prophet of Nazareth were alive again to-day, who would expect to find him at a Lord Mayor's banquet? Would he frequent the Stock Exchange, be at home in the Guild-hall and the Mansion House, or select his disciples from the worshippers in the myriad temples of Mammon? Would he not rather hate and denounce these modern Pharisees as cordially as they would certainly hate and denounce him?

If the City Fathers meant to protect the honor of God, they were both absurd and blasphemous. There is something ineffably ludicrous in the spectacle of a host of fat aldermen rushing out from their shops and offices to steady the tottering throne of Omnipotence. And what presumption on the part of these pigmies to undertake a defence of deity! Surely Omnipotence is as able to punish as Omniscience knows when to punish. The theologians who, as Matthew Arnold says, talk familiarly of God, as though he were a man living in the next street, are modest in comparison with his self-elected body-guard.

Would it not be better for these presumptuous mortals to mind their own business? It will be time enough for them to supervise their neighbors when they have reformed themselves. With all their pretensions to superior piety and virtue, they are notoriously the greatest ring of public thieves in the world, and they are at present lavishly expending trust-monies in a desperate endeavor to justify their turpitude and prolong their plunder.

According to our summons, Mr. Ramsey, Mr. Kemp, and I appeared at the Mansion House on Friday, February 2, 1883. The Justice Room was thronged long before the Lord Mayor took his seat on the Bench, and all the approaches were crowded by anxious sympathisers. All the evidence was of a purely formal character. It was a foregone conclusion that we should be committed for trial. We all three pleaded not guilty and reserved our defence. Before leaving the Court, however, notwithstanding his lordship's interruption, I protested against the revival of an old law which had fallen into desuetude, which had not been enforced in the City of London for over fifty years, and which was altogether alien to the spirit of the age. My remarks were greeted with loud applause by the public in Court. Of course his lordship frowned, and the ushers shouted "Silence!" But the mischief was done. It was obvious that we had many friends, that we were not going to be tried in a hole-and-corner fashion.

Our case excited much interest in London. Most of the newspapers contained a good report of the proceedings at the Mansion House; and even the Tory Evening News, which affirmed that we were three vulgar blasphemers undeserving of notice, had as the leading line on its placard "Prosecution of the Freethinker: Result!"

The Freethinker for February 11 contained an article from my pen on the "Infidel Hunt," and a very admirable article by Mr. Wheeler on "The Fight of Forty Years Ago," narrating the trials of Southwell, Holyoake, Paterson, and other brave heretics. Mr. Ramsey did not then quite approve my attitude of defiance, although he has changed his mind since. He thought it more prudent to bend a little before the storm, instead of daring its utmost violence. He was also anxious to please those with whom he had worked before his partial alliance with me, and who were not prepared to sanction his continued connexion with the Freethinker if he wished to remain with them. For these reasons he retired from our partnership, and I was at once registered as the sole proprietor of the paper. This step naturally added to the danger of my situation, and it was freely used against me at the trial. But I had no alternative, unless the Freethinker was to go down, and that I had resolved to prevent at any cost. At the same time I engaged to take over Mr. Ramsey's business at Stonecutter Street, and to recoup him for his heavy investment; and I am bound to admit that he behaved generously in all these arrangements. On February 11 the following editorial notice appeared in my paper:

> "With this number of the Freethinker I assume a new position. The full responsibility for everything in connexion with the paper henceforth rests with me. I am editor, proprietor, printer and publisher. My imprint will be put on every publication issued from 28 Stonecutter Street, and all the business done there will be transacted through me or my representatives. This exposes me to fresh perils, but it simplifies matters. Those who attack the Freethinker after this week will have to attack me singly. I never meant to give in, and never will so long as my strength serves for the fight. Whoever else yields, I will submit to nothing but physical compulsion. If the Freethinker should ever cease to appear, the Freethought party will know that the fault is not mine. Certain parts of the mechanical process of production are dependent on the firmness of others. One man cannot do everything. But I pledge myself to keep this Freethought flag flying at every hazard, and if I am temporarily disabled I pledge myself to unfurl it again, and if need be again, and again. De l'audace, et encore de l'audace, et toujours de l'audace."

Mr. Wheeler stood loyally by me in this emergency. His efforts for our common object were untiring, and never was his pen wielded more brilliantly. Perhaps, indeed he overstrained his energies, and thus led to the complete breakdown of his health soon after my imprisonment.

A few days later Sir Thomas Nelson, the City Solicitor, served a summons on Mr. H. C. Cattell of 84 Fleet Street, who had so annoyed the bigots by exposing the Christmas Number of the Freethinker in his window. Detectives also visited other newsagents and threatened them with prosecution if they persisted in selling my paper. It was evident that the City authorities were bent on utterly suppressing it. They tried their utmost and they failed.

CHAPTER VI

PREPARING FOR TRIAL

There were many reasons why I did not wish to be tried at the Old Bailey. First, it is an ordinary criminal court, with all the vulgar characteristics of such places: swarms of loud policemen, crowds of chattering witnesses, prison-warders bent on recognising old offenders, ushers who look soured by long familiarity with crime, clerks who gabble over indictments with the voice and manner of a town-crier, barristers in and out of work, some caressing a brief and some awaiting one; and a large sprinkling of idle persons, curious after a fresh sensation and eager to gratify a morbid appetite for the horrible. How could the greatest orator hope to overcome the difficulties presented by such surroundings? The most magnificent speech would be shorn of its splendor, the most powerful robbed of more than half its due effect. In the next place, I should have to appear in the dock, and address the jury from a position which seems to require an apology in itself. And, further, that jury would be a common one, consisting almost entirely of small tradesmen, the very worst class to try such an indictment.

For these and other reasons I resolved to obtain, if possible, a certiorari to remove our Indictment to the Court of Queen's Bench; and as the first Indictment had been so removed, I did not anticipate any serious difficulty. On Monday, February 19, after travelling by the night train from Plymouth, where I had delivered three lectures the day before, I applied before Justices Manisty and Matthew, who granted me a rule nisi. But on the Saturday Sir Hardinge Giffard moved that the rule should be taken out of its order in the Crown Paper, and argued on the following Tuesday. Seeing that the Court was determined to assist him, I acquiesced in the motion rather than waste my time in futile obstruction. On Tuesday, February 27, Sir Hardinge Giffard duly appeared, supported by two junior counsel, Mr. Poland and Mr. F. Lewis. The judges, as on the previous Saturday, were Baron Huddleston and Mr. Justice North. The former displayed the intensest bigotry and prejudice, and the latter all that flippant insolence which he subsequently displayed at my trial, and which appears to be an inseparable part of his character. When, for instance, I ventured to correct Sir Hardinge Giffard on a mere matter of fact, as is quite customary in such cases; when I sought to point out that the Indictment already removed included Mr. Ramsey and myself, and not Mr. Bradlaugh only; Justice North stopped me with "Not a word, sir, not a word."

Sir Hardinge Giffard made a very short speech, knowing that such judges did not require much persuasion. He moved that the rule nisi should be discharged; put in a copy of the Christmas Number of the Freethinker, which he described as a gross and intentional outrage on the religious feelings of the public; alleged, as was perfectly true, that it was still being sold; and urged that the case was one that should be sent for trial at once.

My reply was longer. After claiming the indulgence of the Court for having to appear in person, owing to my purse being shorter than the London Corporation's, I laid before their lordships my reasons for asking them to make the rule absolute. I argued that, as a press offence, our case was eminently one for a special jury; that the law of blasphemy, which had not been interpreted for a generation, was very indefinite, and a common jury might be easily misled; that as contradictory statements of the common law existed, it was highly advisable to have an authoritative judgment in a superior Court; that grave questions as to the relations of the statute and the common law might also arise; that it was manifestly unfair, while a sweeping Indictment for blasphemy was removed to a higher Court, that I should be compelled to plead in a lower Court on a similar charge; and that it was unjust to try our case at the Old Bailey when the City Corporation was prosecuting us.

To none of these reasons, however, did their lordships vouchsafe a reply or extend a consideration. Baron Huddleston simply held the Christmas Number of the Freethinker up in Court, and declared that no sane man could deny that it was a blasphemous libel—a contumelious reproach on our Blessed Savior. But that was not the point at issue. Whether the prosecuted publication was a blasphemous libel or not, was a question for the jury at the proper time and in the proper place. All Baron Huddleston was concerned with was whether a fairer trial might be obtained in a higher Court than in a lower one, and before a special jury than before a common one. That question he never touched, and the one he did touch he was bound by legal and moral rules not to deal with at all.

Justice North briefly concurred with his learned brother, and refrained from adding anything because he would probably have to try the case at the Old Bailey himself. What a pity he did not reflect on the injustice of publicly branding as blasphemous the very men he was going to try for blasphemy within forty-eight hours!

The next morning, February 29, Mr. Ramsey, Mr. Kemp and I duly appeared at the Old Bailey. Before the regular business commenced, I asked his lordship (it was indeed Justice North) to postpone our trial until the next sessions, on the ground that, as my application for a certiorari was only decided the day before, there had been no time to prepare an adequate defence. His lordship refused to grant us an hour for that absurd purpose. Directly I sat down Mr. Poland arose, and begged that our trial might be deferred until the morrow, as his leader, Sir Hardinge Giffard, was obliged to attend elsewhere. This request was granted with a gracious smile and a bland, "Of course, Mr. Poland." What a spectacle! An English judge refusing a fellow-citizen a single hour for the defence of his liberty and perhaps his life, and granting a delay of twenty-four hours to enable a brother lawyer to earn his fee!

I spent the rest of that day in preparations for the morrow—writing out directions for Mr. Wheeler in case I should be sent to prison, arranging books and documents, and leaving messages with various friends; and I sat far into the night putting together finally the notes for my defence. I was quite cool and collected; I neglected nothing I had time for, and I was dead asleep five minutes after I laid my head on the pillow. Only for a moment was I even perturbed. It was when I was giving Mr. Wheeler his last instructions. Pointing to my book-shelves, I said: "Now, Joe, remember that if Mrs. Foote has any need, or if there should ever be a hitch with the paper, you are to sell my books—all of them if necessary." A great sob shook my friend from head to foot. The bitter truth seemed to strike him with startling force. Imprisonment, and all it involved, was no longer a dim possibility: it was a grim reality that might have to be faced to-morrow. "Tut, tut, Joe!" I said, grasping his arm and laughing. But the laugh was half a failure, and there was a suspicious moisture in my eyes, which I turned my face away to conceal.

During the day I had a last interview with Mr. Bradlaugh and Mrs. Besant at 63 Fleet Street. Mr. Bradlaugh told me he could find no flaw in our Indictment, and his air was that of a man who sees no hope, but is reluctant to say so. Mrs. Besant was full of quiet sympathy, proffering this and that kindness, and showing how much her heart was greater than her opportunity of assistance.

In the evening I attended the monthly Council meeting of the National Secular Society. Mr. Ramsey was also present. We both expressed our belief that we should not meet our fellow-councillors again for some time, and solemnly wished them good-bye, with a hope that, if we were sent to prison, they would seize the opportunity, and initiate an agitation against the Blasphemy Laws. I then drove home, and finished the notes for my defence.

Early the next morning I was at 28 Stonecutter Street. Being apprehensive of a fine as well as imprisonment, I made hasty arrangements for removing the whole of the printing plant to some empty rooms in a private house. Mr. A. Hilditch was the friend on whom I relied in this emergency; and I am indebted to him for aid in many other difficulties arising from my prosecution. My foreman printer, Mr. A. Watkin, superintended the removal. By the evening not a particle of our plant remained at the office. Mr. Watkin stuck loyally to his duty during my long absence, and on my return I found how much the Freethinker owed to his unassuming devotion.

One ordeal was left. I had to say good-bye to my wife. It was a dreadful moment. Reticence is wisdom in such cases. I will not inflict sentiment on the reader, and I was never given to wearing my heart upon my sleeve. Let it suffice that I fought down even the last weakness. When I stepped into the Old Bailey dock I was calm and collected. All my energies were strung for one task—the defence of my own liberty and of the rights of Freethought.

That very morning the Freethinker appeared with its usual illustration. It was the last number I edited for twelve months. My final article was entitled, "No Surrender," and I venture to quote it in full, as exhibiting my attitude towards the prosecution within the shadow of the prison walls:—

"The City Corporation is lavishly spending other people's money in its attempt to put down the Freethinker. Sir Thomas Nelson is keeping the pot boiling. He employs Sir Hardinge Giffard and a tail of juniors in Court, and half the detectives of London outside. These surreptitious gentleman, who ought to be engaged in detecting crime, are busily occupied in purchasing the Freethinker, waylaying newsvendors' messengers, intimidating shopkeepers, and serving notices on the defendants. What money, unscrupulously obtained and unscrupulously expended, can do is being done. But there is one thing it cannot do. It cannot damp our courage or alienate the sympathy of our friends.

"There is evidently a widespread conspiracy against us. We have to stand on trial at the Old Bailey in company with rogues, thieves, burglars, murderers, and other products of Christian civilisation. The company is not very agreeable, but then Jesus himself was crucified between two thieves. No doubt the Jews thought him the worst of the three, just as pious Christians will think us worse than the vilest criminal at the Old Bailey; but posterity has reversed the judgment on him, and it will as certainly reverse the judgment on us.

"If a jury should give a verdict against us, which we trust it will not, the prosecutors will probably strike again at some other Freethought publication. The appetite for persecution grows by what it feeds on, and demands sacrifice after sacrifice until it is checked by the aroused spirit of humanity. After a sleep of twenty-five years the great beast has roused itself, and it may do considerable damage before it is driven back into its lair. We may witness a repetition of the scenes of fifty and sixty years ago, when scores of brave men and women faced fine and imprisonment for Freethought, tired out the very malice of their persecutors; and made the Blasphemy Laws a dead letter for a whole generation. May our victory be as great as theirs, even if our sufferings be less.

"But will they be less? Who knows? They may even be greater. Christian charity has grown so cold-blooded in its vindictiveness since the 'pioneer days' that blasphemers are treated like beasts rather than men. There is a certain callous refinement in the punishment awarded to heretics to-day. Richard Carlile, and other heroes of the struggle for a free press, were mostly treated as first-class misdemeanants; they saw their friends when they liked, had whatever fare they could pay for, were allowed the free use of books and writing materials, and could even edit their papers from gaol. All that is changed now. A 'blasphemer' who is sent to prison now gets a month of Cross's plank-bed, is obliged to subsist on the miserable prison fare, is dressed in the prison garb, is compelled to submit to every kind of physical indignity, is shut out from all communication with his relatives or friends except for one visit during the second three months, is denied the use of pen and ink, and debarred from all reading except the blessed Book. England and Russia are the only countries in Europe that make no distinction between press offenders and ordinary criminals. The brutal treatment which was meted out to Mr. Truelove in his seventieth year, when his grey hairs should have been his protection, is what the outspoken sceptic must be prepared to face. After eighteen centuries of Christianity, and an interminable procession of Christian 'evidences,' such is the reply of orthodoxy to the challenge of its critics.

"These things, however, cannot terrorise us. We are prepared to stand by our principles at all hazard. Our motto is No Surrender. What we might concede to criticism we will never yield to menace. The Freethinker, we repeat again, will go on whatever be the result of the present trial. The flag will not fall because one standard-bearer is stricken down; it will be kept flying proudly and bravely as of old—shot-torn and blood-stained perhaps, but flying, flying, flying!"

Let me now pause to say a few words about our Indictment. It was framed on the model of the one I have already described charging us with being wicked and profane persons, instigated by the Devil to publish certain blasphemous libels in the Christmas Number of the Freethinker, to the danger of the Queen's Crown and dignity and the public peace, and to the great displeasure of Almighty God. The various "blasphemies" were set forth in full, and my readers shall know what they were.

Mr. Wheeler's comic "Trial for Blasphemy" was one of the pieces. Matthew, Mark, Luke and John were accused of blasphemy in the Court of Common Sense. They were charged with publishing all the absurdities in the four gospels, and in especial with stating that a certain young Jew was God Almighty himself. After the citation and examination of many witnesses, Mr. Smart, Q.C., urged upon the jury that there was absolutely no evidence against the prisoners. It was perfectly clear that they were not the authors of the libels; their names had been used without their knowledge or sanction; and he confidently appealed to the jury for a verdict of Not Guilty. "After a brief consultation," concluded this clever skit, "the jury, who had carefully examined the documents, were of opinion that there was nothing to prove that the prisoners wrote the libels complained of. A verdict of acquittal was accordingly entered, and the prisoners were discharged."

Now, every person acquainted with Biblical criticism knows that Mr. Wheeler simply put the conclusions of nearly all reputable scholars in a bright, satirical way; and a century hence people will be astonished to learn that such a piece of defensible irony, every line of which might be justified by tons of learning, was included in an indictment for blasphemy, and considered heinous enough to merit severe punishment.

There were a few lines of verse picked out of long poems, and violently forced from their context; and also a few facetious "Answers to Correspondents," mangled in the same way. Certainly any publication could be condemned on this plan. The Bible itself might be proved an obscene book.

Then came eighteen illustrations, entitled "A New Life of Christ." All the chief miracles of his career were satirised, but not a single human incident was made the subject of ridicule. Now, if miracles are not objects of satire, I should like to know what are. If they never happened, why should they enjoy more respect and protection than other delusions? Why should one man be allowed to deny miracles, and another man imprisoned for laughing at them? Must we regard long-faced scepticism as permissible heresy, and broad-faced scepticism as punishable blasphemy? And if so, why not set up a similar distinction between long and broad faces in every other department of thought? Why not let Punch and Fun be suppressed, political cartoons be Anathema, and social satire a felony?

Another illustration was called "A Back View." It represented Moses enjoying a panoramic view of Jahveh's "back parts." Judge North did his dirty worst to misrepresent this picture, and perhaps it was he who induced the Home Secretary to believe that our publication was "obscene." In reality the obscenity is in the Bible. The writer of Exodus contemplated sheer nudity, but the Freethinker dressed Jahveh in accordance with the more decent customs of the age of reason. I would cite on this point the judgment of Mr. Moncure D. Conway, the famous minister of South Place Chapel. He expressed himself as follows in a discourse on Blasphemous Libel immediately after our imprisonment, since published in "Lessons for the Day":—

> *"The prosecutor described the libels as 'indecent,' an ambiguous word which might convey to the public an impression that there was something obscene about the pictures or language, which is not the fact. The coarsest picture is a sidewise view of a giant's form, in laborer's garb, the upper and lower part veiled by a cloud. Only when one knows that the figure is meant for Jahveh could any shock be felt. The worst sense of the word 'indecent' was accentuated by the prosecutor's saying that the libels were too bad for him to describe. In this way they were withheld from the public intelligence while exaggerated to its imagination. The fact under this is that some bigots wished to punish some Atheists, but could only single them out beside eminent men equally guilty, and forestall public sympathy by pretending they had committed a libel partly obscene. This is not English."*

Frederick the Great, being a king, was a privileged blasphemer. In some unquotable verses written after the battle of Rossbach, where he routed the French and drove them off the field pell-mell, he sings, as Carlyle says, "with a wild burst of spiritual enthusiasm, the charms of the rearward part of certain men; and what a royal ecstatic felicity there is in indisputable survey of the same." "He rises," adds Carlyle, "to the heights of Anti-Biblical profanity, quoting Moses on the Hill of Vision." To Soubise and Company the poet of Potsdam sings—

"Je vous ai vu comme Moise
Dans des ronces en certain lieu
Eut l'honneur de voir Dieu."

Frederick's verse is halting enough, but it has "a certain heartiness and epic greatness of cynicism"; and so his biographer continues justifying this royal outburst of racy profanity with Rabelaisian gusto. I dare not follow him; but I am anxious to know why Carlyle's "Frederick" circulates with impunity and even applause, while the Freethinker is condemned and denounced. Judge North may be ignorant of Carlyle's masterpiece, but I can hardly presume the same ignorance in Sir William Harcourt. He probably sinned against a greater light. Few worse outrages on public decency have been committed than his describing my publication as not only blasphemous, but obscene. And the circumstances in which this slander was perpetrated served to heighten its criminality.

CHAPTER VII

AT THE OLD BAILEY

"George William Foote, William James Ramsey, and Henry Arthur Kemp," cried the Clerk of the Court at the Old Bailey. It was Thursday morning, March 1, 1883, and as we stepped into the dock the clock registered five minutes past ten. We were provided with chairs, and there were pens and ink on the narrow ledge before us. It was not large enough, however, to hold all my books, some of which had to be deposited on the floor, and fished up as I required them. Behind us stood two or three Newgate warders, who took quite a benevolent interest in our case. Over their heads was a gallery crammed with sympathisers, and many more were seated in the body of the court. Mr. Wheeler occupied a seat just below me, in readiness to convey any messages or hand me anything I might require. Between us and the judge were several rows of seats, all occupied by gentlemen in wigs, eager to follow such an unusual case as ours. Sir Hardinge Giffard lounged back with a well-practised air of superiority to the legal small-fry around him, and near him sat Mr. Poland and Mr. Lewis, who were also retained by the prosecution. Justice North was huddled in a raised chair on the bench, and owing perhaps to the unfortunate structure of the article, it seemed as though he was being shot out every time he leaned forward. His countenance was by no means assuring to the "prisoners." He smiled knowingly to Sir Hardinge Giffard, and treated us with an insolent stare. Watching him closely through my eye-glass, I read my fate so far as he could decide it. His air was that of a man intent on peremptorily settling a troublesome piece of business; his strongest characteristic seemed infallibility, and his chief expression omniscience. I saw at once that we should soon fall foul of each other, as in fact we did in less than ten minutes. My comportment was unusual in the Old Bailey dock; I did not look timid or supplicating or depressed; I simply bore myself as though I were doing my accustomed work. That was my first offence. Then I dared to defend myself, which was a greater offence still; for his lordship had not only made up his mind that I was guilty, but resolved to play the part of prosecuting counsel. We were bound to clash, and, if I am not mistaken, we exchanged glances of defiance almost as soon as we faced each other. His look said "I will convict you," and mine answered "We shall see."

Sir Hardinge Giffard's speech in opening the case for the prosecution was brief, but remarkably astute. He troubled himself very little about the law of Blasphemy, although the jury had probably never heard of it before. He simply appealed to their prejudices. He spoke with bated breath of our ridiculing "the most awful mysteries of the Christian faith." He described our letterpress as an "outrage on the feelings of a Christian community," which he would not shock public decency by reading; and our woodcuts as "the grossest and most disgusting caricatures." And then, to catch any juryman who might not be a Christian, though perhaps a Theist, he declared that our blasphemous libels would "grieve the conscience of any sincere worshipper of the great God above us." This appeal was made with uplifted forefinger, pointing to where that being might be supposed to reside, which I inferred was near the ceiling. Sir Hardinge Giffard finally resumed his seat with a look of subdued horror on his wintry face. He tried to appear exhausted by his dreadful task, so profound was the emotion excited even in his callous mind by our appalling wickedness. It was well acted, and must, I fancy, have been well rehearsed. Yes, Sir Hardinge Giffard is decidedly clever. It is not accident that has made him legal scavenger for all the bigots in England.

Mr. Poland and Mr. Lewis then adduced the evidence against us. I need not describe their performance. It occupied almost two hours, and it was nearly one o'clock when I rose to address the jury. That would have been a convenient time for lunch, but his lordship told me I had better go on till the usual hour. As I had only been speaking about thirty minutes when we did adjourn for lunch, I infer that his lordship was not unwilling to spoil my defence. How different was the action of Lord Coleridge when he presided at our third trial in the Court of Queen's Bench! The case for the prosecution closed at one o'clock, exactly as it did on our first trial at the Old Bailey. But the Lord Chief Justice of England, with the instinct of a gentleman and the consideration of a just judge, did not need to be reminded that an adjournment in half an hour would make an awkward break in our defence. Without any motion on our part, he said: "If you would rather take your luncheon first, before addressing the jury, do so by all means." Mr. Ramsey, who preceded me then, had just risen to read his address. After a double experience of Judge North, and two months' imprisonment like a common thief under his sentence, he was fairly staggered by Lord Coleridge's kindly proposal, and I confess I fully shared his emotion.

Sir Hardinge Giffard had grossly misled the jury on one point. He told them that even in "our great Indian dominions, where

Christianity was by no means the creed of the majority of the population, it had been found necessary to protect the freedom of conscience and the right of every man to hold his own faith, by making criminal offenders of those who, for outrage and insult, thought it necessary to issue contumelious or scornful publications concerning any religious sect." In reply to this absolute falsehood, I pointed out that the Indian law did not affect publications at all, but simply punished people for openly desecrating sacred places or railing at any sect in the public thoroughfare, on the ground that such conduct tended to a breach of the peace; and that under the very same law members of the Salvation Army had been arrested and imprisoned because they persisted in walking in procession through the streets. Under the Indian law, no prosecution of the Freethinker could have been initiated; and, in support of this statement, I proceeded to quote from a letter by Professor W. A. Hunter, in the Daily News. Judge North doubtless knew that I could cite no higher authority, and seeing how badly his friend Sir Hardinge was faring, he prudently came to his assistance. Interrupting me very uncivilly, he inquired what Professor Hunter's letter had to do with the subject, and remarked that the jury had nothing to do with the law of India. "Then, my lord," I retorted, "I will discontinue my remarks on this point, only expressing my regret that the learned counsel should have thought it necessary to occupy the time of the court with it." Whereat there was much laughter, and his lordship's face was covered with an angry flush.

Later in my address I had a long altercation with his lordship. I wanted to show the jury that such heresy as I had published in the Freethinker abounded in high-class publications, but Justice North endeavoured (vainly enough) to prevent me. The verbatim report of what occurred is so rich that I give it here instead of a summary version:

"Now, gentlemen, I told you before that one of the reasons, in my opinion, why the present prosecution was commenced, was that the alleged blasphemous libels were published in a cheap paper, and I asked you to bear in mind that there was plenty of heresy in expensive books, published at 10s., 12s., and even as much as L1 and more. I think I have a right to ask that you should have some proof of this statement. I think I can show you that similar views are expressed by the leading writers of to-day—not, perhaps, in precisely the same language— for it is not to be expected that the paper which is addressed to the many will be conducted on just the same level, either intellectually or aesthetically speaking, as a publication,

in the form of an expensive book, which is only intended for men of education, intelligence and leisure; but such views are put before the public by the most prominent writers of the day. You will, of course, expect to find differences in the mode of expression, and as a matter of course, differences of taste; but I submit that differences of taste affect the question very little unless, as I have said, they actually lead to breaches of the peace. But in a case like this there ought to be no distinction on grounds of taste. Surely the man who says a thing in one way is not to be punished, while the man who says the same thing in another way is to go scot free. You cannot make a distinction between men on grounds of taste. I can imagine that if there were a parliament of aesthetic gentlemen, and Mr. Oscar Wilde were made Prime Minister, some such arrangement as that would find weight before the jury; but, in the present state of enlightened opinion, I do not think that any such arrangement would be accepted by you. Now, gentleman, I shall call your attention first of all to a book which is published by no less a firm than the old and well-established house of Longmans. The author of the book——

Mr. Justice North: What is the name of the book?

Mr. Foote: The book is the 'Autobiography of John Stuart Mill.'

Mr. Justice North: What are you going to refer to it for?

Mr. Foote: I am going to refer to one page of it, my lord.

Mr. Justice North: What for?

Mr. Foote: To show that identical views to those expressed in the cheap paper before the court are expressed in expensive volumes.

Mr. Justice North: I shall not hear anything of that sort. I am not trying the question, nor are the jury, whether the views expressed by other persons are sound or right. The question is whether you are guilty of a blasphemous libel. I shall direct them that it will be for them to say whether the facts are proved in this case.

Mr. Foote: I will call your attention, my lord, to the remarks of Lord Justice Cockburn in a similar case.

Mr. Justice North: I will hear anything relevant to the subject.

My reason for asking you was to find out whether you were going to quote a law book.

Mr. Foote: I will quote a verbatim report.

Mr. Justice North: I can hear that.

Mr. Foote: It is the case against Charles Bradlaugh and Annie Besant.

Mr. Justice North: By whom is your report published?

Mr. Foote: It is a verbatim report published by the Freethought Publishing Company—the shorthand notes of the full proceedings, with the cross-examination and the judgment of the court.

Mr. Justice North: There is no evidence of that. Did you hear it?

Mr. Foote: I did not personally hear it, but my co-defendants did.

Mr. Justice North: I will hear you state anything you suggest as being said by Lord Chief Justice Cockburn.

Mr. Foote: Mrs. Besant was about to read a passage from 'Tristram Shandy'——

Mr. Justice North: You have not proved the publication.

Mr. Foote: Quite so, my lord; but although this is not formal evidence, and only the report of a case, I thought your lordship would not object to hear it.

[Mr. Foote here handed in a copy of the report to the judge, and pointed out that the Lord Chief Justice had said he could not prevent Mrs. Besant from committing a passage to memory, or from reading books as if reciting from memory].

Mr. Justice North: I will allow you to go on, either quoting from memory or reading from the book; but I cannot go into the question of whether this is right or not.

Mr. Foote: I am not proposing that. I am only going to show that opinions like those expressed here extensively prevail.

Mr. Justice North: That is not the question at all. If they extensively prevail, so much the worse. What somebody else has said, whoever that person may be, cannot affect the question in this case.

Mr. Foote: But, my lord, might it not affect the question of whether a jury might not themselves, by an adverse verdict, be far more contributing to a breach of the peace than the publication on which they are asked to adjudicate?

Mr. Justice North: I think not, and it shall not do so if I can help it. It is a mere waste of time to attempt to justify anything that has been said in the alleged libel by showing that someone else has said the same thing.

Mr. Foote: In all trials the same process has been allowed.

Mr. Justice North: It will not be allowed on this occasion.

Mr. Foote: If your lordship will pardon me for calling attention to the famous case of the King against William Hone, I would point out that there Hone read extracts to the jury.

Mr. Justice North: Very possibly it might have been relevant in that case.

Mr. Foote: But, my lord, it was precisely a similar case—it was a case of blasphemous libel. Lord Ellenborough sat on the bench.

Mr. Justice North: Possibly.

Mr. Foote: And Lord Ellenborough allowed Mr. Hone to read what he considered justificatory of his own publication. The same thing occurred in the case of the Queen against Bradlaugh and Besant.

Mr. Justice North: We have nothing to do to-day with the question whether any author has taken the views which are taken in these libels, whoever the author was.

Mr. Foote: Does your lordship mean that I am to go on reading or not?

Mr. Justice North: Go on with your address to the jury, sir; that's what I wish you to do. But you cannot do what you were about to do—refer to the book you mentioned for any such purpose as you indicated.

Mr. Foote: I hope your lordship does not misunderstand me. I am simply defending myself against a very grave charge under an old law.

Mr. Justice North: Go on, go on, Foote. I know that. Go on with your address.

Mr. Foote: Your lordship, these questions are part of my address. Gentlemen (turning to the jury), no less a person than a brother of one of our most distinguished judges has said——

Mr. Justice North: Now, again, I cannot have you quoting books not in evidence, for the sake of putting before the jury the matters they state. The passage you referred to is one in which the Lord Chief Justice pointed out that that could not be done.

Mr. Foote: But the action, my lord, of the Lord Chief Justice did not put a stop to the reading. He said he would allow Mrs. Besant to quote any passage as a part of her address.

Mr. Justice North: Go on.

Mr. Foote: No less a person than the brother of one of our most learned——

Mr. Justice North: Now did I not tell you that you could not do that?

Mr. Foote: Will your lordship give me a most distinct ruling in this case?

Mr. Justice North: I am ruling that you cannot do what you are trying to do now.

Mr. Foote: I am sorry, my lord, I cannot understand.

Mr. Justice North: I am sorry for it. I have tried to make myself clear.

Mr. Foote: Does your lordship mean that I am not to read from anything to show justification of the libel?

Mr. Justice North: There is no justification in the case. The question the jury have to decide is whether you, and the persons present with you, are guilty of a libel or not. For that purpose they will have to consider whether the matters in question are a libel. If so, they will have also to consider whether you and the other defendants are guilty of having published it. If they think it a libel, and that you have published it, they will have answered the only two questions they will have to put to themselves.

Mr. Foote: My lord, in an ordinary libel case justification can be shown.

Mr. Justice North: Go on.

Mr. Foote: I do not wish to occupy the time of the court unnecessarily, but really I think your lordship ought to remember the grave position in which I stand, and not stand in the way of anything which I consider to be of vital importance to my defence.

Mr. Justice North: I have pointed out to you what I consider to be the question the jury have got to decide. I hope you will not go outside the lines I have pointed out to you; but, with these remarks, I am very reluctant to interfere with any prisoner saying anything which he considers necessary, and I will not stop you. I hope you will not abuse the concession I consider I am making to you.

Mr. Foote: I should be very sorry, my lord. I am only stating what I consider necessary."

This is a very fair specimen of his lordship's manners. Unfortunately, it is also a fair specimen of his lordship's law. When I read similar extracts in the Court of Queen's Bench, Lord Coleridge never interrupted me once; nay, he told the jury that I had very properly brought those passages before their notice, that I had a perfect right to do so, and that it was a legitimate part of my defence. Since then I have conversed with many gentlemen who were present, some of them belonging to the legal profession, and I have heard but one opinion expressed as to Judge North's conduct. They all agree that it was utterly undignified, and a scandal to the bench. Perhaps it had something to do with his lordship's removal, a few weeks afterwards, to the Chancery Court, where his eccentricities, as the Daily News remarked at the time, will no longer endanger the liberty and lives of his fellow-subjects.

When I cited Fox's Libel Act and asked that my copy, purchased from the Queen's printers, might be handed to the jury for their guidance, his lordship sharply ordered the officer not to pass it to them. "I shall tell them," he said, "what points they have to decide," as though I had no right to press my own view. He would never have dared to treat a defending counsel in that way, and he ought to have known that a defendant in person has all the rights of a counsel, the latter having absolutely no standing in court except so far as he represents a first party in a suit. "May they not have a copy of the Act, my lord?" I inquired. "No," replied his lordship, "they will take the law from the directions I give them; not from reading Acts of Parliament." This is directly counter to the spirit and letter of Fox's Act; and I suspect that Judge North would have expressed himself more guardedly in a higher court. If juries have nothing to do with Acts of Parliament, why are statutes enacted? Judge North would be ashamed and afraid to speak in that way before his superior brother judges at the Law Courts; but at the Old Bailey he was absolute master of the situation, and he abused his power. He knew there was no court of criminal appeal, and no danger of his being checked by either of the fat aldermen on the bench. They were in fact our prosecutors, and they appeared to enjoy their paltry triumph.

As I have said, I began my address to the jury at one o'clock, and at half-past we adjourned for lunch. Mr. Wheeler ran across the road and ordered some refreshment for us, and pending its arrival we descended the dock-stairs and entered a subterranean passage, which was lit by a single gas-jet. On each side there was a little den with an iron gate. One of these was filled with prisoners awaiting trial or sentence, who gazed through the bars at us with mingled glee and astonishment. They were chatting merrily, and I imagine from their free and easy manner that most of them were old gaol-birds. Perhaps there were some forlorn, miserable creatures cowering in the darkness behind, with throbbing brows and hearts like lead, on whose ears the light laughter of their callous companions grated even more harshly than it did on ours.

The left-hand den was empty, and into it we were ushered by the aged janitor, who regarded us with looks of mute reproach. He was evidently subdued to what he worked in. His world consisted of two classes—criminals and police; and without any further ceremony of trial and sentence, the very fact of our descending into his Inferno was clear evidence that we belonged to the former class.

As the den was only illuminated by a few straggling gleams from the gas-jet outside, we were unable to discriminate any object until our eyes grew accustomed to the gloom. While we were in this state of semi-blindness, something stirred. I wondered whether it was a dog or a rat. The doubt was soon resolved. A human form reared itself up from the bench against the wall, where it had been lying, not asleep indeed, but half unconscious; and to our great surprise, it turned out to be Mr. Cattell, who had surrendered to his bail at the same time as we did, and had been shivering there ever since ten o'clock. After we left him he continued shivering for three or four hours longer in that black-hole of the Old Bailey, which struck a chill into our very bones even in the brief period of our tenancy, and which could hardly be warmed by any conflagration short of the last. It appeared damp as well as cold, and a sinister effluvium came from a place of necessity at the back. Six or seven hours' incarceration in such a place might injure a strong constitution and seriously damage a weak one. Surely it is scandalous that unconvicted prisoners, some of whom are eventually acquitted, should suffer this unnecessary hardship and incur this unnecessary risk.

Presently our lunch arrived. The platefuls of meat and vegetables had a savory smell, our appetites were keen, and our stomachs empty. But a difficulty arose. There were forks, but no knives; those lethal instruments being forbidden lest prisoners should attempt to cut their throats. I subsequently had the use of a tin knife in Newgate, but even that, which used to be common in prisons, is now proscribed. The only carving instruments allowed the guests in her Majesty's hotels is a wooden spoon, although the tin knife still lingers in the Houses of Detention. Among other elaborate precautions against suicide, I found that the prisoners awaiting trial were furnished with quill pens. Steel pens had been banished after the desperate exploit of one poor wretch, who had stabbed away at his windpipe with one, and inflicted such grave injuries that the officials had great difficulty in saying his life.

But revenons a nos moutons, or rather our forks. We disposed of the vegetables somehow, and as for the meat, we were obliged to split and gnaw it after the fashion of our primitive ancestors. We drank out of the mouth of the claret bottle, passing it round till it was emptied. It was probably a good honest bottle, but in the circumstances it seemed a despicable fraud. We tried hard for another supply, but we failed. Being anxious to prevent a display of inebriety in the dock, or desirous to repress rather than stimulate our audacity, the venerable janitor interposed the most effectual obstacles, and we were constrained to reason down the remnant of our thirst, which, if I may infer from my own case, was almost as insensible to argument as the judge himself.

Feeling very cold, we essayed a little exercise. The dimensions of our den, which were three steps each way, did not allow much play for individuality. Erratic pedestrianism was clearly dangerous, so we rushed round in Indian file, like braves on the warpath; and, by way of relieving the tedium, we speculated on the number of laps in a mile. Our proceedings seemed to strike the wild beasts in the opposite den as unaccountable imbecility. They grinned at us through the bars with as much delight as children might evince in the Zoological Gardens at a performance of insane monkeys. But their amusement was suddenly arrested. St. Peter appeared at the gate, flourishing his keys. It was two o'clock.

What a strange sensation it was, mounting those dock stairs! More loudly than my experiences below, it said—"You are a prisoner." The court was densely crowded, and as I emerged into it, the sea of faces, suddenly caught en masse, seemed cold and alien. The feeling was only momentary, but I fancy it resembled the weird thrill that must have swept through the ancient captive as he entered the Roman arena from his dark lair, and confronted the vague host of indifferent faces that were to watch his fight for life.

I resumed my address to the jury at two o'clock, and concluded it at four. A considerable portion of that time was spent in altercations with the judge, of which I have already given some striking specimens. Let me now give another. It excited great laughter in court, and I confess the situation was so comic that I could scarcely preserve my own gravity. After quoting a number of "blasphemous" passages from the writings of Professor Clifford, Lord Amberley, Matthew Arnold, the author of "The Evolution of Christianity," Swinburne, Byron and Shelley, I proceeded thus: "Now, gentlemen, I have given you a few illustrations of permitted blasphemy in expensive books, and I will now trouble you with a few instances of permitted blasphemy in cheap publications, which are unmolested because they call themselves Christian, and because those who conduct them are patronised by ecclesiastical dignitaries." Here I produced a copy of the War Cry, in which I had marked a piece of idiotic "blasphemy." Judge North scented mischief, and gestured to the officer behind me. But that functionary was too deeply interested in the case to make much haste, and, not wishing to be frustrated, I read as rapidly as I could. Before he could arrest me I had finished the extract. My auditors were all convulsed with laughter, except the judge, who was convulsed with rage. As soon as he could articulate he addressed me as follows:

> Mr. Justice North: Now, Foote, I am going to put a stop to this. I will not allow any more of these illustrations of what you call permitted blasphemy in cheap publications. I decline to have any more of them put before me.
>
> Mr. Foote: My Lord, I will use them for another purpose, if you will allow me.
>
> Mr. Justice North: You will not use them here at all, sir.
>
> Mr. Foote: May they not be used, my lord to show that an equally free use of religious symbols, and religious language, prevails widely in all classes of literature and society?
>
> Mr. Justice North: No they may not. I decline to hear them read. They are not in evidence, and I refuse to allow you to quote from such documents as part of your speech.
>
> Mr. Foote: Well, gentlemen, I will now ask your attention very briefly to another branch of the subject.

The fact is, I was perfectly satisfied. I had purposely kept the War Cry till the last. It naturally ended my list of citations, and his lordship's victory was entirely specious.

Those who may wish to read my address in its entirety will find it in "The Three Trials for Blasphemy." For those, however, who are not so curious or so painstaking, I give here the peroration only, to show what sentiments I appealed to in the breasts of the jury, and how far my defence was from boastfulness or servility:

> "Gentlemen,—I told you at the outset that you, are the last Court of Appeal on all questions affecting the liberty of the press and the right of free speech and Freethought. When I say Freethought, I do not refer to specific doctrines that may pass under that name: I refer to the great right of Freethought, that Freethought which is neither so low as a cottage nor so lofty as a pyramid, but is like the soaring azure vault of heaven, which over-arches both with equal case. I ask you to affirm the liberty of the press, to show by your verdict that you are prepared to give to others the same freedom that you claim for yourselves. I ask you not to be misled by the statements that have been thrown out by the prosecution, nor by the authority and influence of the mighty and rich Corporation which commenced this action, has found the money for it, and whose very solicitor was bound over to prosecute. I ask you not to be influenced

> by these considerations, but rather to remember that this present attack is made upon us probably because we are connected with those who have been struck at again and again by some of the very persons who are engaged in this prosecution; to remember that England is growing day by day in its humanity and love of freedom; and that, as blasphemy has been an offence less and less proceeded against during the past century, so there will probably be fewer and fewer proceedings against it in the next.
>
> Indeed, there may never be another prosecution for blasphemy, and I am sure you would not like to have it weigh on your minds that you were the instruments of the last act of persecution—that you were the last jury who sent to be caged like wild beasts men against whose honesty there has been no charge. I am quite sure you will not allow yourselves to be made the agents of sending such men to herd with the lowest criminals, and to be subjected to all the indignities such punishment involves.
>
> I am sure you will send me, as well as my co-defendants, back to our homes and friends, who do not think the worse of us for the position in which we stand: that you will send us, back to them unstained, giving a verdict of Not Guilty for me and my co-defendants, instead of a verdict of Guilty for the prosecution; and thus, as English juries have again and again done before, vindicate the glorious principle of the freedom of the press, against all the religious and political factions that may seek to impugn it for their own ends."

The court officials could not stifle the burst of applause that greeted my peroration. I had flung all my books and papers aside and faced the jury. I spoke in passionate accents. My expression and gestures were doubtless full of that dramatic power which comes of earnest sincerity. I felt every sentiment I uttered, and I believe I made the jury feel it too, for they were visibly impressed, and their emotion was obviously shared by the crowd of listeners who represented the greater jury of public opinion.

Mr. Ramsey followed me with a speech which he read from manuscript. It occupied half an hour in delivery. It was terse and vigorous, and it really covered most of the ground in debate. I listened to it with pleasure as an admirable summary of our position. But it lost much of its force in being read instead of spoken extemporaneously, and its very virtues as a paper were its defects as an address. The points wanted elaboration. Before they had fairly mastered one argument, the jury were hurried on to another. Mr. Ramsey is by no means incapable of making a forcible speech, and I think he should have trusted to his power of improvisation. There was no need for a long effort. He might have concentrated himself on a few salient points of our defence, and pressed them on the jury with all his might. His own sentiments, naturally expressed, in homely language, would have had a greater effect than any literary composition. After an experience of three trials, I would give this advice to every man who has to defend himself before a jury on a charge of blasphemy or sedition—"Write out on a sheet of paper the heads of your defence. Number them in the order you think they should be treated, so that your address may have a logical continuity. Fill in your sub-divisions, similarly numbered, under the chief heads, beginning the lines half-way across the page, so as to catch the eye readily. Think every clause out carefully. Fix every illustration in your mind until it becomes almost a fact of memory. Don't write out fine passages and try to remember them verbally. Write nothing; it will only confuse you, unless you have long practised that method. When you have systematised your thoughts, and think your written arrangement is complete, ponder it clause by clause with the paper at hand for constant reference. No matter if your thoughts seem to wander, and the subject appears to grow vague; your mind is dwelling on it, and ideas will fructify in your mind unconsciously as seeds sprout in the dark. When the hour of trial arrives, arm yourself with the familiar paper, trust to your own courage, and speak out. You will have thoughts, and nature will find you words."

Justice North's summing-up was simply a clever and unscrupulous bit of special pleading. Sir Hardinge Giffard had left the court, and his friend on the bench conducted his case for him. He told the jury that I had wasted their time, and indulged in a number of other insults, which might be pardonable in a legal hack bent on earning his client's fee, but were scarcely consistent with the dignity and impartiality of a judge. His tone was even worse than his words. He had no sympathy with us in our desperate effort to defend our liberty against such overwhelming odds, nor did we solicit any; but we had a right to expect him to refrain from constant expressions of antipathy. That, however, was not the whole of his offence against the rules of justice. He recurred to the bad old example of Lord Ellenborough in devoting most of his time to answering my arguments. Lord Coleridge remarked in the Court of Queen's Bench that such a task was not for the judge, but for the counsel on the other side of the case. I wish his lordship had read a lesson to Justice North on that subject before he presided at our trial.

There is only one passage of his summing-up that I wish to criticise fully. It contains his statement of the Law of Blasphemy. But as he made a very different statement four days later on at our second trial, I prefer to wait until, by placing these discrepant utterances together, I can give the reader a fair idea of Justice North's authority as a legal oracle.

The jury retired at five o'clock. Justice North kept his seat, probably fancying they would soon agree to a verdict of Guilty. But as the minutes went by, and the result seemed after all dubious, he resorted to a paltry trick. Notwithstanding the late hour, he had Mr. Cattell brought into the dock for trial. By procuring a verdict against him our jury might be influenced. According to theory, of course, the jury hold no communication with the world while in deliberation; but it is well known that officers of the court have access to them, and tidings of Mr. Cattell's fate could be easily conveyed.

We stepped down the stairs, out of sight but not out of hearing, and made way for Mr. Cattell to take our place in the dock. He was very pale with cold and apprehension, and too timid to take a seat, he stood with his hands resting on the top ledge. The evidence against him was very brief. Instead of defending himself he had employed counsel. That gentleman admitted the "horrible character of the publication, so eloquently denounced by the learned judge." He said that his client could not for a moment think of defending it; in fact, he had only sold it in ignorance, and he would never repeat the offence. On the ground of that ignorance and that promise, it was hoped that the jury would return a verdict of Not Guilty. Mr. Cattell declares that he never instructed his counsel to say anything of the kind; but all I know is that it was said, and that while our cheeks were tingling with shame and indignation, he heard it all without a word of protest.

Judge North acted openly as counsel for the prosecution in this trial. There was not the slightest disguise. He took the case completely into his own hands, examined and cross-examined. His summing-up was a disgusting exhibition. Naturally enough the jury returned a verdict of Guilty without leaving the box; but sentence was deferred until our jury had also agreed.

By this time, I felt convinced they would not agree, and every minute strengthened my belief. While they deliberated we were all conducted to the subterranean den, where we kept each other in good spirits. St. Peter brought us some water to drink in a dirty tin can. We tasted it, found that a little of it was more than enough, and declined to hazard a further experiment on our health. At last, after two hours and ten minutes' waiting, we were summoned back to the dock. There was profound silence in court, and as the jury filed into their seats a painful sense of expectation pervaded the assembly. His lordship said that he had called them into court to see whether he could assist them in any way, and especially by explaining the law to them again. The foreman, in a very quiet, composed manner, replied that they all understood the law, but there was no chance of their agreeing. His lordship invited them to try a further consultation, to which the foreman replied that it would be useless. "Then," said his lordship, "I am very sorry to say I must discharge you, and have the case tried again." Then, turning to the Clerk of Arraigns, he added, "I will attend here on Monday and try the case again with a different jury." This was against the ordinary rule of the court, and the sessions had to be prolonged into the next week for our sakes; but his lordship could not deny himself the luxury of sentencing us. He had set his heart on sending us to gaol, and would not be baulked.

We naturally expected to be liberated till Monday, and I formally applied for a renewal of our bail. But his lordship refused my application in the most peremptory and insulting manner. I pointed out that I should require a proper opportunity to prepare another defence for the second trial, to which his lordship replied, "You will have the same opportunity then that you have now." He then hurriedly left the bench, and we were in custody of the Governor of Newgate. Several friends rushed forward to shake hands with us over the dock rail, and there were loud cries of "Bravo, jury!" Presently we descended to the Inferno again, from which we were conducted by a long subterranean passage to Newgate prison.

Judge North's action was simply vindictive. Even if we were guilty our offence was only a misdemeanor. We had been out on bail from the beginning of the prosecution, we had duly surrendered to trial, after the jury's disagreement we really stood in a better position than before, and there was not the slightest reason to suppose that we might abscond. On the other hand, it was clear that we were fighting against long odds. The rich City Corporation was prosecuting us regardless of expense, and their case was conducted by three of the most skilful lawyers in London. Reason, justice and humanity, alike demanded that we should enjoy freedom and comfort while marshalling our resources for a fresh battle. Judge North, however, thought otherwise; in his opinion we required a different kind of "opportunity." He locked us up in a prison cell, excluded us from light and air, deprived us of all communication with each other, and debarred us from all intercourse with the outside world except during fifteen minutes each day through an iron grating. Such malignity is an unpardonable crime in a judge. There may have been some bad criminals in Newgate when I entered it, but I would rather have embraced the worst of them than have touched the hand of Judge North.

CHAPTER VIII

NEWGATE

The subterranean passage through which Mr. Ramsey, Mr. Kemp, Mr. Cattell, and I were conducted from the Old Bailey dock to Newgate prison, was long and tortuous, and two or three massive doors were unlocked and relocked for our transit before we emerged into the courtyard. In the darkness the lofty walls looked grimly frowning, and I imagined what feelings must possess the ordinary criminal who passes under their black shadow to his first night's taste of imprisonment. Another massive door was opened in the wall of Newgate, and we were ushered into what at first sight appeared a large hall. It was really the interior of the prison. Glancing up, I saw dimly-lighted corridors, running round tier on tier of cell-doors, and connected by light, graceful staircases; a clear view of every door being commanded from the office at the west end of the ground-floor.

We were invited one by one into a side office, where we inscribed our names in a big book. A dapper little officer, who treated me with a queer mixture of authority and respectfulness, wrote out my description as though he were filling in a passport. I was very much amused, and finding he was not too precise in his observations, I corrected and supplemented them in a good-humored manner.

After completing this task he requested me to deliver up the contents of my pockets. Having passed nearly all my money to Mr. Wheeler, I had little to deposit. Some prisoners, however, are less careful. The officer told me that he occasionally received as much as ten or twelve pounds from one visitor, although the majority were almost penniless. My small change was carefully counted by us both, and when it was stowed in my purse, I put my signature under the amount in the register.

Then followed my other belongings. I had stupidly brought a bunch of keys, which the officer eyed very suspiciously. Keys in a prison! The official mind might well be alarmed. Next came some letters and telegrams I had received while in Court, and a lead pencil, which I took from my breast-pocket.

"Anything more in that pocket?" said the officer, catching hold of the coat-lappet, and attempting to insert his hand.

"I beg pardon," I replied, disengaging his hand and stepping back; "I can do that myself. See!" I said, turning my pocket inside out.

He was satisfied, but slightly annoyed. The man was simply doing his duty, and I daresay he showed me far more courtesy than other prisoners were treated with. Yet the process of searching is unspeakably revolting, and I shrank from it instinctively; taking care, however, by my rapid gestures to render it unnecessary.

Prisoners are regularly searched in Holloway Gaol, as well as in other penal establishments; and being under the ordinary prison regulations, like other "convicted criminals," I was of course subjected to the indignity. I must in candor admit that the officers made it as little offensive as possible in my case; yet the touch of a man's hand about one's person is so repulsive, that I always had great difficulty in suppressing my indignation. If an officer owes a prisoner a grudge, he is able (especially if the man is a little more refined than the general run of his associates) to render the searching an almost intolerable infliction. Sometimes the prisoners are stripped to their drawers or shirts, without any particular reason; and the process can even be carried farther, until they are in a state of complete nudity. On one occasion this experiment was attempted on me, but I declined to submit to it, and the brace of officers (they always search in pairs, to prevent collusion) shrank from employing force.

All the requisite formalities being transacted, I was supplied with a pair of sheets and a duster; and carrying these on my arm, I was conducted upstairs to my apartment. Before leaving, however, I shook hands with my companions, although it was in direct defiance of the "rules and regulations."

My cell was Number One. It was considered the place of honor. I was informed that it was once tenanted by the elder of two famous brother forgers, who spent three weeks there preparing his defence and writing an extraordinary number of letters. This information was communicated to me with an air of solemnity as though so eminent a criminal had left behind him the flavor of his greatness, and had in some measure consecrated the spot.

The gas was lit, and the officer withdrew, banging the door as he went. He seemed to love the sound, and I subsequently discovered that this was a characteristic of his tribe. Only two men in Holloway Gaol ever shut my door gently. They were the gallant Governor and a clerical locum tenens who officiated during the chaplain's frequent absence in search of recreation or health. Colonel Milman closed the door like a gentleman. Mr. Stubbs closed it like an undertaker. He was the most nervous man I ever met. But I must not anticipate. More of him anon.

Prison cells, I had always known, are rather narrow apartments, but the realisation was nevertheless a rough one. My domicile, which included kitchen, bedroom, sitting-room and water-closet, was about ten feet long, six feet wide, and nine feet high. At the end opposite the door there was a window, containing perhaps three square feet of thick opaque glass. Attached to the wall on the left side was a flap-table, about two feet by one, and under it a low stool. In the right corner, behind the door, were a couple of narrow semi-circular shelves, containing a wooden salt-cellar full of ancient salt, protected from the air and dust by a brown paper lid, through which a piece of knotted string was passed to serve as a knob. The walls were whitewashed, and hanging against them were a pair of printed cards, which on examination I found to be the dietary scale and the rules and regulations. The floor was black and shiny. It was probably concreted, and I discovered the next day that it was blackleaded and polished. Finally I detected an iron ring in each wall, facing each other, about two feet from the ground. "What are these for?" I thought. "They would be convenient for hanging if they were three feet higher. Perhaps they are placed there to tantalise desperate unfortunates who might be disposed to terminate their misery and wish the world an eternal 'Good Night!'"

As I paced up and down my cell, full of the thought, "I am in prison, then," my curiosity was excited by a large urn-looking object in the right corner under the window, just below a water-tap and copper basin. I had noticed it before, but I fancied it was some antique relic of Old Newgate. Examining it closely, I found it had a hinged lid, and on lifting this my nose was assailed by a powerful smell, which struck me as about the most ancient I had ever encountered. This earthenware fixture was in reality a water-closet, and I imagined it must have communicated direct with the main drainage. A more unwholesome and disgusting companion in one's room is difficult to conceive. I believe these filthy monstrosities still exist in Newgate, although they are abolished in other prisons. Yet it puzzles one to understand why prisoners awaiting trial should be poisoned by such a diabolical invention any more than prisoners who have been convicted and sentenced.

Just as I finished inspecting this monument of official ingenuity, I heard a heavy footstep along the corridor, and presently a key was inserted in my lock. It "grated harsh thunder" as it turned. The door was flung open abruptly, without any consideration whether I might be standing near it, and an official entered, who turned out to be the chief warder. He was a polite, handsome man of five-and-forty, with a fine pair of dark eyes and a handsome black beard. During my brief residence in Newgate he treated me with marked civility, and sometimes engaged in a few minutes' conversation. In one of these brief interviews he told me that he had officiated at fourteen executions, and devoutly hoped he might never witness another, his feelings on every occasion having been of the most horrible character. I also found that he was fond of a book, although he had little leisure for reading or any other recreation. He looked longingly at my well-printed copy of Byron; but what impressed him most was my little collection of law books, especially Folkard's fat "Law of Libel," which he regarded with the awe and veneration of a bibliolater, suddenly confronting a gigantic mystery of erudition.

This worthy officer came to tell me that my "friend with the big head" had just called to see what he could do for us. "Big-head" was Mr. Bradlaugh. The description was facetious but by no means uncomplimentary. Our meals had been ordered in from "over the way," and I might expect some refreshment shortly. While he was speaking it was brought up. He then left me, and I devoured the coffee and toast with great avidity. My appetite was far from appeased, but I had to content myself with what was given me, for prison warders look as surprised as Bumble himself at a request for "more."

When the slender meal was dispatched, the chief warder paid me another visit to instruct me how to roost. Under his tuition I received my first lesson in prison bed-making. A strip of thick canvas was stretched across the cell and fastened at each end by leather straps running through those mysterious rings. A coarse sheet was spread on this, then a rough blanket, and finally a sieve-like counterpane; the whole forming a very fair imitation of a ship's hammock. It had by no means an uncomfortable appearance, and being extremely fagged, I thought I would retire to rest. But directly I essayed to do so my troubles began. When I tried to get on the bed it canted over and deposited me on the floor. Slightly shaken, but nothing daunted, I made another attempt with a similar result. The third time was lucky. I circumvented the obstinate enemy by mounting the stool and slowly insinuating myself between the sheets, until at length I was fairly ensconced, lying straight on my back like a prone statue or a corpse. For a few moments I remained perfectly still enjoying my triumph. Presently, however, I felt rather cold at the feet, and on glancing down I saw that my lower extremities were sticking out. I raised myself slightly in order to cover them, but the movement was fatal; the bed canted and I was again at large. This time I had serious thoughts of sleeping on the floor, but as it was hard and cold I abandoned the idea. I laboriously regained my lost position, taking due precautions for my feet. After a while I grew accustomed to the oscillation, but I had to face another evil. The clothes kept slipping off, and more than once I followed in trying to recover them. At last, I found a firm position, where I lay still, clutching the refractory sheets and blankets. But I soon experienced a fresh evil. The canvas strip was very narrow, and as my shoulders were not, they abutted on each side, courting the cold. Even this difficulty I finally conquered by gymnastic subtleties. Warmth and comfort produced their natural effect. My brain was busy for a few minutes. Thoughts of my wife and the few I loved best made me womanish, but a recollection of the malignant judge hardened me and I clenched my teeth. Then Nature asserted her sway. Weary eyelids drooped over weary eyes, and through a phantasmagoria of the trial I gradually sank into a feverish sleep.

I was aroused in the morning by the six o'clock bell. It was pitch dark in my cell except for the faint glimmer of a distant lamp through the thick window-panes. A few minutes later a little square flap in the centre of my door was let down with a startling bang; a small hand-lamp was thrust through the aperture, and a gruff voice cried "Now, then, get up and light your gas: look sharp." I cannot say that I made any indecent haste. My gas was lit very leisurely, and as I returned the lamp I saw a scowling visage outside. The man was evidently exasperated by my "passive resistance."

My ablutions were performed in a copper basin not much larger than a porridge bowl; indeed, it was impossible to insert both hands at once. There was, of course, no looking-glass, and as the three-inch comb was densely clogged with old deposits, my toilet was completed under considerable difficulties. I never combed my hair with my fingers before, but on that occasion I was obliged to resort to those primitive rakes.

When I was finally ready, the chief warder summoned me downstairs to be weighed and measured. My height was five feet ten in my shoes, and my weight twelve stone nine and a half in my clothes.

At eight o'clock breakfast came. It consisted of coffee, eggs and toast. At half-past eight we were taken out to exercise. What a delight it was to see each other's faces again! And how refreshing to breathe even the atmosphere of a City courtyard after being locked up for so many hours in a stifling cell.

The other prisoners were already outside, and we had to pass through the court in which they were exercising to reach the one considerately allotted for our special use. They presented a cheerless spectacle. Silently and sadly, with drooping heads, they skirted the walls in Indian file; a couple of officers standing in the centre to see that no communication went on between them. Many eyes were lifted to gaze at us as we passed. Some winked, and a few looked insolent contempt, but the majority expressed nothing but curiosity.

Our courtyard was about thirty feet by twenty. It was stone-paved, with a door leading to the Old Bailey at one end, and a row of high iron bars at the other. The air was brisk, and the sky tolerably clear for the place and season. Our pent-up energies required a vent, and we rushed round like caged animals suddenly loosened. "Gently," cried our good-natured custodian; but we paid little heed to his admonition; our blood was up, and we raced each other until we were wearied of the pastime.

Presently I heard my name called, and on advancing to the spot whence the voice issued, I saw Mr. Bradlaugh's face through the iron bars. After a few minutes' conversation he made way for Mrs. Besant. She was quite unprepared for such an interview. Her idea was that she would be able to shake hands; I, however, knew better, and for that reason I had forbidden my wife to visit me, preferring her letters to her company in such wretched circumstances. Mrs. Besant was particularly cordial. "We are all proud," she said, "of the brave fight you made yesterday." How the time slipped by! When she retired it seemed as though our conversation had but just opened.

I was only entitled to receive two visitors, but by a generous arithmetic Mr. Bradlaugh and Mrs. Besant were counted as one. Mr. Wheeler was therefore able to see me on business. We had much to arrange, and the result was that I enjoyed scarcely more than half an hour's exercise. Surely it is a grievous wrong that a prisoner awaiting trial should be allowed such brief interviews with his friends, especially when he is defending himself, and may require to consult them. And is it not a still more grievous wrong that these interviews should take place during the exercise hour? There is no reason why they should not be kept separate; indeed there is no reason why the inmates of Newgate should not be allowed to exercise twice a day. No work is done in the prison, and marshalling the prisoners is not so laborious a task that it cannot be performed more than once in twenty-four hours.

At the expiration of our miserable sixty minutes we were marched back to our cells; but we were scarcely under lock and key again before we were summoned to the Old Bailey, the officer telling us that he thought they were going to grant us bail. We were conducted through the subterranean passage to the Old Bailey dock-stairs. Standing out of sight, but not out of hearing, we listened to Mr. Avory's application for bail on behalf of Mr. Kemp. Judge North refused in cold, vindictive tones; he had evidently let the sun go down on his wrath, and rise on it again. Mr. Avory thereupon asked whether he made no difference between convicted and unconvicted prisoners. "None in this case," was his lordship's brutal and supercilious answer; and then we were hurried back to our cells.

My apartment was execrably dark. It was situated in an angle of the building; there was a wall on the right and another in front, so that only a little light fell on the right wall of my cell near the window. After severely trying my eyes for two or three hours, I was obliged to make an application for gas, which, after some hesitation, was granted. But I found the remedy almost worse than the evil. Sitting all day at the little lap-table, with my head about ten inches from the gas-light, made me feel sick and dizzy. Mr. Ramsey, as I afterwards discovered, was made quite ill by a similar nuisance, and the chief warder was obliged to release him for a brief walk in the open air. I applied the next morning for a fresh cell, and was duly accommodated. My new apartment was very much lighter, but the change was in other respects a disadvantage. The closet was fouler, and as the lid was a remarkably bad fit, it emitted a more obtrusive smell. The copper basin also was filled with dirty water, which would not flow away, as the waste-pipe was stopped up. To remedy these defects they brought the engineer, who strenuously exercised his intellect on the subject for three days; but as he exercised nothing on the waste-pipe, I insisted on having the copper basin baled out, and secured a bucket for my ablutions.

During my first day in Newgate, the officers occasionally dropped in for a minute's chat with such an unusual prisoner. I found them for the most part "good fellows," and singularly free from the bigotry of their "betters." The morning papers also helped to wile away the time. I was pleased to see that the Daily News rebuked the scandalous severity of the judge, and that the reports of our trial were reasonably fair, although very inadequate. The Daily Chronicle was under an embargo, and could not be obtained for love or money; the reason being, I believe, that many years ago it commented severely on some prison scandal, and provoked the high and mighty Commissioners into laying their august proscription upon it. All the weekly papers, or at least the Radical ones I inquired for, were under a similar embargo, for what reason I could never discover. Perhaps the Commissioners, who enjoy a reputation for piety, exclude Radical and heterodox journals lest they should impair the Christianity and Toryism of the gaol-birds.

Many letters reached me and were answered, so that my time was well occupied until twelve, when dinner was brought in from "over the way." Being well-nigh ravenous, I dispatched it with great celerity, washing it down with a little mild ale. Prisoners awaiting trial are allowed (if they can pay for it) a pint of that beverage, or half a pint of wine.

After dinner I felt drowsy, and as there was no sofa or chair, and no back to the little three-legged stool, I was obliged to dispense with a nap. I walked up and down my splendid hall instead, longing desperately for a mouthful of fresh air by way of dessert, or a few minutes' chat with my friends, who I dare say were in exactly the same predicament.

Tea, which came at five, brightened me up, and as Mr. Wheeler had by this time sent in all my books and papers, I settled down to three hours' hard work. The worthy Governor, a tall sedate man, did not like the titles of some of my books, and inquired whether I really wanted them for my defence. I replied that I did. "Then," said he to the chief warder, "they may all be brought up, but you must take care they don't get about." At half-past eight, according to the rules, I retired to my precarious and uncomfortable couch; a few minutes later my gas was turned off, and I was left in almost total darkness to seek the sleep which I soon found. Thus ended my first day in Newgate.

My second day in Newgate passed like the first. Prison life affords few variations; the days roll by with drear monotony like wave after wave over a spent swimmer's head. We enjoyed Judge North's "opportunity" to prepare our fresh defence in the way I have already described. We were locked up in our brick vaults twenty-three hours out of the twenty-four; we walked for an hour after breakfast in the courtyard; and the fifteen minutes allowed for the "interview with two visitors" was, as before, religiously deducted from the sixty minutes allowed for "exercise." Mr. Wheeler sent in more books and papers, and I devoted my whole time, except that occupied in answering letters, to preparing another speech for Monday.

Sunday was a miserably dull day. No visits are allowed in that sacred interval, a regulation which presses with great severity on the poorer prisoners, whose relatives and friends are freer to visit them on Sunday than during the week.

The confinement was beginning to tell on me. My life had

been exceptionally active, physically and mentally, and this prison life was as stagnant as the air of my cell. Thus "cabin'd cribbed, confined," I felt all my vital functions half arrested. Dejection I did not experience; my spirits were light and fresh; but the body revolted against its ill-treatment, and recorded its protest on the conscious brain.

How grateful was the brief hour's exercise on the Sunday morning! The muffled roar of the great city was hushed, and the silence served to emphasise every visual phenomenon. Even the air of that city courtyard, hemmed in by lofty walls, seemed a breath of Paradise. I threw back my shoulders, expanding the chest through mouth and nostrils, and lifted my face to the sky. A pale gleam of sunshine pierced through the canopy of London smoke. It might have looked ghastly to a resident in the country, unused to the light London calls day, but to one immured in a prison cell it was an irradiation of glory. The mind expanded under the lustre; imagination preened its wings, and sped beyond the haze into the everlasting blue.

Gallant Lovelace, in durance vile, boasted his unfettered mind, and sang—

> *"Stone walls do not a prison make,*
> *Nor iron bars a cage."*

True, but the model prison was not invented then, nor was the silent system in vogue. Lovelace's apartment was, perhaps, not so scrupulously clean as mine, but it commanded a finer prospect. He knew nothing of the horror of opaque windows, and his iron bars did not exclude the air and light.

At eleven o'clock my cell door was opened, and an officer asked me if I would like to go to chapel. "Yes," I replied, for I was curious to see what a religious service in Newgate was like, and any interruption of the day's monotony was welcome.

Standing outside my cell door, I perceived Mr. Ramsey, Mr. Kemp, and Mr. Cattell already outside theirs. The few other prisoners still remaining in Newgate (they are transferred to other prisons as soon as possible after sentence) were ranged in a similar manner. A file was then formed, and we marched, accompanied by officers, through a passage on the ground floor to the chapel, passing on our way the glass boxes in which prisoners hold communication with their solicitors. An officer stands outside during the interview: he can hear nothing, but he is able to see every motion of the occupants; the object of this mechanism being to guard against the passage of any interdicted articles.

The chapel was small, lighted by a large window on the left side from the door, and warmed by a mountainous stove in the centre. A few backless forms were provided on the floor for unconvicted prisoners. We were accommodated with the front bench, and requested to sit two or three feet apart from each other, the few other prisoners occupying seats behind us being separated in the same way. The convicted prisoners sit in a railed-off part of the chapel, and I believe there is a gallery for the women. On our right, facing the window, was a pulpit, below which was the clerk's desk, flanked on the right by the Governor's box and on the left by a seat for the officers.

After waiting some time, we heard footsteps at the door. In strode the tall Governor and the Chaplain, the one entering his box, and the other going to the clerk's desk, where he read the service, which was rushed through at the rate of sixty miles an hour. Mr. Duffeld started the hymns, but his voice is not melodious, and he has little sense of tune. The singing, indeed, would have broken down if it had not been for the Francatelli of the establishment, who had exchanged his kitchen costume for the official uniform, and sang with the fervor and emphasis of a Methodist leader or a captain in the Salvation Army.

Mr. Duffeld mounted the pulpit to read his sermon. His text was Matthew vii., 21: "Not everyone that saith unto me Lord, Lord, shall enter into the kingdom of heaven; but he that doeth the will of my father which is in heaven." This text caused me a pleasant surprise. I had heard of Mr. Duffeld as a member of, or a sympathiser with, the Guild of St. Matthew; and I fancied that he meant to condemn our prosecution, not directly, so as to offend his employers, but indirectly, so as to justify himself and satisfy us. I was, however, greviously mistaken. Mr. Duffeld's sermon was directed against the large order of "professing Christians," who manage a pretty easy compromise between God and Mammon, between Jesus Christ and the world and the flesh, if not the Devil. It had no reference to us, and it was entirely inappropriate to the rest of the congregation, who, I must say, from the casual glimpses I caught of them, were glancing about aimless as monkeys, or staring listless like melancholy monomaniacs.

When the benediction was pronounced, Mr. Duffeld marched swiftly away; the tall Governor strode after him, and the prisoners filed in silence through the doorway back to their cells. What a commentary it was on "Our Father!" It was a ghastly mockery, a blasphemous farce, a satire on Christianity infinitely more sardonic and mordant than anything I ever wrote or published. Soon after returning to my cell I was glad of the substantial dinner and drowsy ale to deaden the bitter edge of my scorn.

After tea I settled down to the final preparations for my defence. My gas was left on for an extra hour to afford me the time I required. It was half-past nine when I retired to my hammock. Everything was then finished except the interview I had requested with my co-defendants. This the Governor was powerless to grant. He had applied to the visiting magistrates, who protested the same inability. A "petition" had then been forwarded to the Home Secretary, but no answer had been received. While I was pondering this difficulty, my cell door was suddenly opened, and the Governor entered. Apologising for disturbing me unceremoniously at that unseasonable hour, he informed me that a messenger from the Home Office had brought the necessary permission for our interview. It took place the next morning. We had just thirty minutes to arrange our plan for the approaching battle, the consultation being held in the courtyard before breakfast. The time was of course absurdly inadequate. We had a just claim to better treatment, Mr. Ramsey, Mr. Kemp and I; we were charged with the same offence; we pleaded to a common indictment; we stood together in the same dock; we were involved in the same fate; and witnesses would be called against us all three indifferently. Surely, then, as the jury had disagreed once, and we had to defend ourselves afresh, we were entitled to proper conference with our papers before us. This al fresco chat was the last of Judge North's "opportunities." At ten o'clock we were once more in the Old Bailey dock, fronting the judge and jury, surrounded by an eager crowd, and beginning a second fight for liberty and perhaps for life.

CHAPTER IX

THE SECOND TRIAL

Before I had been in the Old Bailey dock two minutes on the morning of my second trial, I found that our case was hopeless. The names of no less than four jurymen were handed to me by friends in court, every one of whom had been heard to declare that he meant to bring in a verdict of Guilty. One of these impartial guardians of English liberty had stated, in a public-house, his intention to "make it hot for the Freethinkers." How many more had uttered similar sentiments it is impossible to say, but it is reasonable to suppose that, if four were discovered by my friends, there were others who had escaped their detection. One of the four, a Mr. Thomas Jackson, was called on the jury list. I at once challenged him. He was then put into the witness-box, and on examination he admitted that he "had expressed an opinion adverse to the defendants in this case."

Then ensued a bit of comedy between Judge North and Sir Hardinge Giffard, who both assumed a wonderful air of impartiality.

Judge North: Sir Hardinge, is it not better to withdraw this juryman at once? Whatever the verdict of the jury, I should be sorry to have a man among them who had expressed himself as prejudiced.

Sir Hardinge Giffard: Oh yes, my lord; I withdraw him. It will be much more satisfactory to the Crown and everybody else concerned."

"I withdraw him," says Sir Hardinge; "I should be sorry to have him," says the Judge; both evidently feeling that they were making a generous concession in the interests of justice. But as a matter of fact they had no choice. Mr. Thomas Jackson could no more sit on that jury after my challenge than he could fly over the moon. I smiled at the pretended generosity of these legal cronies, and said to myself, "Thank you for nothing."

Mr. Thomas Jackson's exit made no practical difference. I felt, I will not say that the jury was packed, but that it was admirably adapted to the end in view. Ours being the only case for trial that day, it was not difficult to accomplish this result. A friend of mine said to one of the officers of the court before I entered the dock, "Well, how is the case going to-day?" "Oh," was the prompt reply, "they are sure to convict." He knew the character of the jury.

Some of the "twelve men and true" had not even the decency to attend to the proceedings. One was timed by a friend in court—dead asleep for sixty minutes. When that juryman awoke his mind was made up on the case. At the conclusion of a trial that lasted over six hours they did not even retire for consultation. They stood up, faced each other, muttered together for about a minute, nodded their heads affirmatively, and then sat down and gave a verdict of guilty.

Several of the jury, however, I am bound to admit, had no idea that Judge North would inflict upon us such infamous sentences, and they were quite shocked at the consequences of their verdict. Four of them subsequently signed the memorial for our release. A fifth juryman vehemently declined to do so. "No," he said, "not I. I'm a man of principle! They got off too easy. Two years' hard labor wouldn't have been a bit too much." This pious gentleman is a publican in Soho, and bears the name of a famous murderer, Wainwright.

But to return. Mr. Ramsey and I were represented this time on all legal points by counsel. Mr. Cluer watched our interests vigilantly, and performed a difficult task with great courage and judgment. He bore Judge North's insults with wonderful patience. "Don't mind what you think about, it, Mr. Cluer," "I don't want you to tell me what you think;" such were the flowers of courtesy strewed from the bench upon Mr. Cluer's path. Our counsel's colleague in the case was Mr. Horace Avory, who represented Mr. Kemp. He also had a somewhat onerous duty to perform.

There is no need to deal with the technical evidence against us. It was of the usual character, and we merely cross-examined the witnesses as a matter of form. One thing was brought out clearly. Sir Henry Tyler's solicitors were aiding Sir Thomas Nelson, and their clerks were produced as witnesses against us.

Judge North's reception of evidence was peculiar. Knowing that there was no Court of Criminal Appeal, he set the rules of procedure at defiance. Any tittle-tattle was admitted, and postmen and servants were allowed to swear as to the directions on unproduced documents alleged to have been addressed to me. When, several weeks later, I was tried a third time in the Court of Queen's Bench, I heard Lord Coleridge rebuke the prosecuting counsel for attempting to put questions against which Judge North would hear no objection. I understand now how much prisoners are at the mercy of judges, and I feel how much truth there was in the remark I once heard from a prisoner in Holloway Gaol, that "it's often a toss up whether you get one year or seven."

Let me here also ask why Mr. Fawcett, the late Postmaster General, allowed his letter-carriers to be employed as detectives in such a case. It was proved in evidence that a policeman had called at the West-Central Post Office, and obtained an interview with the manager, after which the letter-carriers were instructed to spy upon my correspondence. Mr. Fawcett subsequently denied that the letter-carriers had ever been so instructed; but in that case the Post Office witnesses must have committed perjury. I do not believe it. I am confident that they merely obeyed orders, and that the scandalous abuse of a public trust must be charged upon the district postmaster, who probably thinks any weapon is legitimate against Freethinkers. As Mr. Fawcett refused to censure the postmaster for exceeding his duty, or the letter-carrier for committing perjury, I cannot hold him altogether guiltless in the matter.

In opening my defence I took care to accentuate my appreciation of Judge North's kindness, as the following passage will show:

"Gentlemen of the Jury,—I stand in a position of great difficulty and disadvantage. On Thursday last I defended myself against the very same charges in the very same indictment. The case lasted nearly seven hours, and the jury retired for more than two hours without being able to come to an agreement. They were then discharged, and the learned judge said he would try the case again on Monday with a new jury. As I had been out on bail from my committal, and as I stood in the same position after that abortive trial as before it commenced, I asked the learned judge to renew my bail, but he refused. I pleaded that I should have no opportunity to prepare my defence, and I was peremptorily told I should have the same opportunity as I had had that day. Well, gentlemen, I have enjoyed the learned judge's opportunity. I have spent all the weary hours since Thursday, with the exception of the three allowed for bodily exercise during the whole interval, in a small prison cell six feet wide, and so dark that I could neither write nor read at midday without the aid of gaslight. There was around me no sign of the animated life I am accustomed to, nothing but the loathsome sights and sounds of prison life. And in these trying and depressing circumstances I have had to prepare to defend myself in a new trial against two junior counsel and a senior counsel, who have had no difficulties to contend with, who have behind them the wealth and authority of the greatest and richest Corporation in the world, and who might even walk out of court in the

perfect assurance that the prosecution would not be allowed to suffer in their absence."

Those who wish to read the whole of my defence, which lasted over two hours, will find it in the "Three Trials for Blasphemy." One portion of it, at least, is likely to be of permanent interest. With Mr. Wheeler's aid I drew up a long list of the abusive epithets applied by Christian controversialists to their Pagan opponents or to each other. It fills more than two pages of small type, and pretty nearly exhausts the vocabulary of vituperation. I added a few pearls of orthodox abuse of Atheism, and then asked the jury whether Christians had taught Freethinkers to show respect for their opponents' feelings. "Nobody in this country," I continued, "whatever his religion, is called upon to respect the feelings of anybody else. It is only the Freethinker who is told to respect the feelings of people from whom he differs. And to respect them how? Not when he enters their places of worship, not when he stands side by side with them in the business and pleasures of life, but when he reads what is written for Freethinkers without knowing that a pair of Christian eyes will ever scan the page."

It may be asked why I adopted a course so little likely to conciliate my judges. My reply is that I did not try to conciliate them. Feeling convinced that their verdict was already settled, and that my fate was sealed, I cast all such considerations aside, and deliberately made a speech for my own party. I was resolved that my loss should be the gain of Freethought. The peroration is the only other part of my defence I shall venture to quote. It ran as follows:

"Gentlemen, carry your minds back across the chasm of eighteen centuries and a half. You are in Jerusalem. A young Jew is haled along the street to the place of judgment. He stands before his judge; he is accused—of what, gentlemen? You know what he is accused of—the word must be springing to your lips—Blasphemy! Every Christian among you knows that your founder, Jesus Christ, was crucified after being charged with blasphemy. Gentlemen, it seems to me that no Christian should ever find a man guilty of blasphemy after that, but that the very word ought to be wiped from your vocabulary, as a reproach and a scandal. Christians, your founder was murdered as a blasphemer, for, although done judicially, it was still a murder. Surely then you will not, when you have secured the possession of power, imitate the bad example of those who killed your founder, violate men's liberties, rob them of all that is perhaps dearest to them, and brand them with a stigma of public infamy by a verdict from the jury-box!

Surely gentlemen, it is impossible that you can do that! Who are we? Three poor men. Are we wicked? No, there is no proof of the charge. Our honor and honesty are unimpeached. It is not for us to play the Pharisee and say that we are better than other men. We only say that we are no worse. What have we done to be classed with thieves and felons, dragged from our homes and submitted to the indignities of a life so loathsome and hideous, that it is even revolting to the spirits of the men who have to exercise authority within the precincts of the gaol? You know we have done nothing to merit such a punishment. Gentlemen, you ought to return a verdict of Not Guilty against us, because the prosecution have not given you sufficient evidence as to the fact; because whatever legal bigotry is gained from the decisions of judges in the past must be treated as obsolete, as the London magistrate treated the law of Maintenance; because we have done nothing, as the indictment states, against the peace; because our proceedings have led to no tumult in the streets, no interference with the liberty of any man, his person or property; because no evidence has been tendered to you of any malice in our case; because there is no wicked motive in anything we have done; because the founder of your own creed was murdered on a very similar charge to that of which we stand accused now; and, lastly, because you should in this third quarter of the nineteenth century assert once and for ever the great principle of the absolute freedom of each man, unless he trench on the equal freedom of others. I ask you to assert the great principle of the liberty of the press, liberty of the platform, liberty of thought and liberty of speech; I ask you to prevent such prosecutions as are hinted at in the Times this morning; I ask you not to allow sects once more to be hurling anathemas against each other, and flying to the magistrates to settle questions which should be settled by intellectual and moral suasion; I ask you not to open a discreditable chapter of English history that ought to have been closed for ever; I ask you to give us a verdict of Not Guilty, to send us back to our homes and to stamp your brand of disapprobation on this prosecution, which is degrading religion by associating it with all that is penal, obstructive, and loathsome; I ask you to let us go away from here free men, and so make it impossible that there ever should again be a prosecution for blasphemy; I ask you to have your names inscribed in history as the last jury that decided for ever that great and grand principle of liberty which is broader than all the skies; a principle so high that no temple could be lofty enough for its worship; that grand principle which should rule over all—the principle of the equal right and the equal liberty of all men. That is the principle I ask you to assert by your verdict of Not Guilty. Gentlemen, I ask you to close this discreditable chapter of persecution once and for ever, and associate your names on the page of history with liberty, progress, and everything that is dignified, noble and dear to the consciences and hearts of men."

When I sat down there was a burst of applause, which the court officials were unable to suppress. Mr. Ramsey followed with another written speech, well composed and very much to the point. I noticed some of his auditors outside the jury-box choking down their emotion as he touchingly referred to his sleepless nights in Newgate through thinking of wife and child. His Lordship, I observed only smiled bitterly.

Judge North's summing up was a fraudulent performance. He told the jury that the consent of the Attorney-General had to be obtained for our prosecution, as well as that of the Public Prosecutor, which was a downright falsehood, unless it was a piece of sheer ignorance. He pretended to read the whole chapter on Offences against Religion in Sir James Stephen's "Digest of the Criminal Law," while in reality he deliberately omitted the very paragraph which damned his contention and supported mine. He also produced a new statement of the Law of Blasphemy to suit the occasion. On the previous Thursday he told the jury that any denial of the existence of Deity or of Providence was blasphemy. But in the meantime the public press had condemned this interpretation of the law as dangerous to high-class heretics. His lordship, therefore, expounded the law afresh, so as to exempt them while including us. The only question he now submitted to the jury was, "Are any of those passages put before you calculated to expose to ridicule, contempt or derision the Holy Scriptures or the Christian religion?" This amended statement of the Law of Blasphemy went directly in the teeth of our Indictment, which charged us with bringing Holy Scripture and the Christian Religion into disbelief as well as contempt. The fact is, blasphemy is a judge-made crime, and the "blasphemer's" fate depends very largely on who tries him. Lord Coleridge holds one view of the law, Sir James Stephen another, and Justice North another still. Nay, the last judge differs even from himself. He can give two various definitions of the law in five days, no doubt on the principle that circumstances alter cases, and that what is true for one purpose may be false for another.

I have said that the jury, with indecent haste, returned a verdict of Guilty. The crowd of people in court were evidently surprised at the result, although I was not, and they gave vent to groans and hisses. The tumult was indescribable. Suddenly there rang out from the gallery overhead the agonising cry of my young wife, whom I had implored not to come, and whose presence there I never suspected. She had crept in and listened all day to my trial, never leaving her seat for fear of losing it; and now, overwearied and faint for want of food, she reeled under the heavy blow. My heart leaped at the sound; my brain reeled; the scene around me swam in confusion—judge, jury, lawyers and spectators all shifting like the pieces in a kaleidoscope; my very frame seemed expanding and dissolving in space. The feeling lasted only a moment. Yet to me how long! With a tremendous effort I crushed down my emotions, and the next moment I was mentally as calm as an Alp, although physically I quivered like a race-horse sharply reined up in mid-gallop by an iron hand. My wife I could not help, but I could still maintain the honor and dignity of Freethought.

Order was at length restored after his lordship had threatened to clear the court. Mr. Avory then asked him to deal leniently with Mr. Kemp, who was merely a paid servant of ours, and in no other way actually responsible for the incriminated publication. Justice North listened with ill-concealed impatience. He was obviously anxious to flesh the sword of justice in his helpless victims. Directly Mr. Avory finished he began to pronounce the following sentence on me, and while he spoke there was deadly silence in that crowded court:—

"George William Foote, you have been found Guilty by the jury of publishing these blasphemous libels. This trial has been to me a very painful one. I regret extremely to find a person of your undoubted intelligence, a man gifted by God with such great ability, should have chosen to prostitute his talents to the service of the Devil. I consider this paper totally different from any of the works you have brought before me in every way, and the sentence I now pass upon you is one of imprisonment for twelve calendar months."

Twelve months! It was longer than I expected, but what matter? My indifference, however, was not shared by the crowd. They rose, and as the reporter said, "burst forth into a storm of hissing, groaning, and derisive cries." "Damn Christianity!" I heard one shout, and "Scroggs" and "Jeffries" were flung at the judge, who seemed at first to enjoy the scene, although he grew alarmed as the tumult increased. "Clear the gallery," he cried, and the police burst in among the people. But before they did their work something happened. From the first I resolved, if I were found guilty and sentenced to imprisonment, that I would say something before leaving the dock. My first impulse was to hurl at the judge a few words of passionate indignation. But I reflected "No! I have been tried and condemned for ridiculing superstition. Sarcasm is Blasphemy. Well then, let me sustain my character to the end. I will leave with a stinging Freethinker sentence on my lips." Raising my hand, I obtained a moment's silence. Then I folded my arms and surveyed the judge. Our eyes flashed mutual enmity for a few seconds, until with a scornful smile and a mock bow I said, "Thank you, my lord; the sentence is worthy of your creed."

That retort has frequently been cited. It was a happy inspiration, and the more I ponder it the more profoundly I feel that it was exactly the right thing to say.

The officers behind gave me a pressing invitation to descend the dock stairs, and I complied. For a long time I waited in one of the little dens I have already described, pacing up and down, revolving many thoughts, and wondering what detained my companions. The fact is, the police had a great deal of trouble in executing the judge's orders, and some time elapsed before he could strike Mr. Ramsey and Mr. Kemp. Meanwhile I could hear through the earth and the brick walls the roar of that indignant crowd which filled the street and suspended traffic, and I knew it was the first sound of public opinion reversing my unjust sentence.

Consider it for a moment. There is no allusion to outraged feelings, much less any suggestion of "indecency." It is a plain declaration of theological hatred; it breathes the spirit which animated the Grand Inquisitors when they sentenced heretics to be burnt to ashes at the stake. "Listen," says the judge. "I am on God's side. You are on the Devil's. God doesn't see you, but I do; God doesn't punish you, but I will. We have hells on earth for you Freethinkers, in the shape of Christian gaols, and to hell you go!"

Presently Mr. Ramsey came down with nine months on his back, and then Mr. Kemp with three. They had my sentence between them. Mr. Cattell afterwards joined us without any sentence. He was ordered to enter into his own recognisances in L200, and to find one surety in L100, to come up for judgment when called upon.

People have wondered on what principle Judge North determined our sentences. One theory is that he punished us according to the amount of his time we occupied. I made a long speech and got twelve months; Mr. Ramsey made a short speech and got nine; Mr. Kemp made no speech and got only three; while Mr. Cattell cried Peccavi and got off with a caution.

"Ready," cried the old janitor, in response to a distant voice. Our den was unlocked and we were marched back to Newgate for the last time.

CHAPTER X

"BLACK MARIA"

When we entered Newgate as "condemned criminals," we were theoretically under severe discipline, but the officers considerately allowed us a few minutes' conversation in the great hall before we marched to our cells. We shook hands with Mr. Cattell, whom I rather contemptuously congratulated on his good fortune. He went into the office to receive back his effects, and that was the last we saw of him. Vanishing from sight, he vanished from mind. During my imprisonment I scarcely ever thought of him in connexion with our case, and in writing this history I have had to tax my memory to record his insignificant role.

According to the "rules and regulations," all our privileges ended on our sentence. We were therefore entitled to nothing but prison fare after leaving the Old Bailey. But the hour was late, the cook was probably off duty, and our tea and toast had been waiting for us since five o'clock; so the head warder decided that we might postpone our trial of the prison menu until the morning. When it was brought to me, my toast (to use an Hibernicism) proved to be bread-and-butter. There were three slices. I ate two, but could not consume the third, my appetite being spoiled by excitement and the tepid tea.

The officer who acted as waiter informed me that the Old Bailey Street had been thronged all the afternoon, and was still crowded. "We all thought," he said, "that you would get off after that speech—and you would have with another judge. But you won't be in long. They're sure to get you out soon." I shook my head. "Take my word for it," he answered. Thanking him for his kindness, I told him I had no hope, and was reconciled to my fate. Twelve months was a long time, but I was young and strong, and should pull through it. "Yes," he said, with an appreciative look from head to feet, "there isn't much the matter with you now. But you'll be out soon, sir, mark my word."

I have learnt since that the crowd waited to give Judge North a warm reception. But they were disappointed. His lordship went home, I understand, via Newgate Street, and thus baffled their enthusiasm. Mr. Cattell was, I believe, less fortunate. He was hooted and jeered by the multitude, and obliged to take ignominious shelter in a cab.

Strange as it may seem, my last night in Newgate was one of profound repose. I was wearied, exhausted; and spent nature claimed an interval of rest. For a few minutes I lay in my hammock, listening to the faint sound of distant voices and footsteps. Memory and fancy were inert; only the senses were faintly alive. Consciousness gradually contracted to a dim vision of the narrow cell, then to a haze, in which the gaslight shone like a star, and finally died out. But by one of those fantastic tricks the imps of dreaming play us, the last patch of consciousness changed into my wife's face. It was too dim and distant to stir grief or regret; like the vague vision of a beloved face hovering over eyes that are waning in death.

In the morning I was awakened as usual by the officer bringing the light for my gas. At eight o'clock the little square flap in my door was let down with the customary bang, and, on looking through the aperture, I perceived a big pan containing a curious clotted mixture, which resembled bill-stickers' paste. Behind the utensil I saw part of an officer's uniform. This worthy stirred the mixture with a ladle, while he jocosely inquired, "D'ye want any of this?" I did not. "Come," he continued, "put out your tin and I'll give you some." I told him my appetite was not robust enough for his hospitality, and he passed on, probably feeling sure I should not eat the prison fare, and thinking the stuff too good to be wasted. I took the little brown loaf he offered me and examined it closely. It was very hard, and apparently very dry. Depositing it on the shelf, I breakfasted on cold water and the slice of bread-and-butter left over night.

After this sumptuous repast I was let out for exercise. This time the three "condemned" blasphemers were not taken to a separate court. We paraded the common yard with the other prisoners. They were few in number, but they showed many varieties of disposition. One hung his head, and doggedly tramped round the wretched enclosure; another walked erect and stiff, with an air of defiance; another shuffled along with a vacant stare, as though dazed by his fate; another looked as indifferent as though he were walking along the street; and another leered at his companions in misfortune, as though the whole thing were an elaborate joke. For a few minutes I trotted behind Mr. Ramsey, with whom I exchanged a few cheerful words, but the vigilant officers soon separated us. "How long have ye got?" was the constant question of the man at my rear, until the officers detected, and removed him. I was surprised and annoyed at this easy familiarity, but I grew accustomed to it afterwards. The rules of civilised society naturally lapse in prison.

Talking is strictly prohibited, "pals" are rigorously kept apart, nobody knows who will be next him in the exercise ring, and any man who wants to wag his tongue must strike up a conversation with his immediate neighbor. "How long are ye doing?" is almost invariably the introduction. This muttered question brings a muttered answer. Confidences are exchanged, and the conversation grows animated, until at last the speakers forget prudence, and betray themselves to the eyes or ears of an officer, who immediately parts them, or makes them both fall out, and reports them to the Governor for violating the rules. The old stagers acquire a knack of talking without moving their lips, so that the words just reach the man in front or behind. If an officer suspects one of these worthies, he calls out, "Now then, seventeen, I see ye!" "See me what?" says the indignant innocent. "Talking," replies the officer. "Why, I never opened my lips," says the prisoner, and his defence is perfectly true.

On returning from the exercise yard to our cells, we were furnished with a sheet of paper and an envelope to write the last letter which "condemned criminals" are permitted to send from prison after their sentence. The privilege is almost a mockery, for no answer is allowed, and there is little consolation in flinging a final word into the vast silence, which seems deaf because unresponsive. A last interview, however brief, would be far more merciful.

We were summoned from our cells at eleven o'clock for conveyance to Holloway Gaol. All our effects were handed over to us, and we formally signed a receipt for them in the big book. While this process was going on the officers allowed us to chat, and endeavoured to console us by insisting that we should "soon be out." One of them, with a practical turn of mind, recollecting that I had complained of my apartment, informed me that there were some beautiful cells at Holloway.

Having pocketed our belongings, we were conducted through the subterranean passage I have several times mentioned to the great courtyard. The head-warder conversed with us very genially, but when we emerged into daylight and faced the prison van drawn up to receive us, his manner changed. Holding a formidable document, he called out our names and descriptions, officially satisfying himself that we were the persons under sentence. I told him, with mock solemnity, that I had no doubt I was the George William Foote described on the blue paper, and my fellow prisoners gave him a similar assurance.

It was a critical moment. Will they, I thought, try to handcuff us? I hoped not, for I had resolved not to submit tamely to any gratuitous indignities, and I should have felt it necessary to offer what resistance I could to such a flagrant insult. Happily the handcuffs were kept out of sight. One by one we ascended the steps, entered the narrow passage in the van, and huddled ourselves into the narrower boxes. They were so small that no ordinary-sized man could sit upon the little bench at the back. I was obliged to crouch on one ham diagonally, my shoulders stretching from corner to corner. Half a dozen holes were bored through the floor, and there was a space between the side of the box and the roof of the van, which sloped away like an eave. Probably the ventilation was ample, yet I felt stifled, and so powerful is imagination that I breathed heavily and irregularly. But reason soon came to my assistance and allayed my apprehensions, although a remnant of fancy still speculated on what would happen if the vehicle upset.

Presently the door was banged, and "Black Maria" started with her living freight. We had the conveyance, or rather its interior, all to ourselves. Surely the boxes we were pent in never held such company before. Three "blasphemers," who had never injured man, woman or child, were travelling to gaol under a collective sentence of two years' imprisonment, for no other crime than honestly criticising a dishonest creed. We were going to spend weary days and months among the refuse of society. We were doomed to associate with the criminality which still curses civilisation, after eighteen centuries of the gospel of redemption. Posterity would condemn our sentence as a crime, but meanwhile we were fated to suffer.

Rattle, rattle, rattle! How the wretched machine did rattle! Even the roar of the streets we traversed was inaudible, quenched in the frightful din. All I could do was to inspect the memorials of my predecessors in that box. The sides were scrawled over with their names (or nicknames) and sentences. Their brief observations had a jovial tone. I suppose the miserable passengers in that black ferry-boat to Hades are too full of care to indulge in such trifling, and only wanton larrikins and old stagers employ their pencils in illustrating the planks.

After a long drive we entered an archway and stopped. A heavy door was closed behind us, and another opened in front. The van moved forward a few yards and turned round. Then the door was opened, and looking out I saw the front of Holloway Gaol.

Several minutes elapsed before we descended from the prison van. During this interval I chatted freely with my fellow-prisoners, although we could not see each other. But I have always found, as one of George Meredith's characters says, that observation is perhaps the most abiding pleasure in life, and I watched with great amusement the antics of a sprucely-dressed young fellow who sat on the step behind, and held a facetious conversation with the pleasant officer who "delivered" us at Holloway. This natty blade was, I presumed, our driver. His talk was of horses and drinking, and I wondered how he obtained the money to purchase all the liquors which he boasted of having imbibed that morning. He seemed to possess a sort of right divine to enjoyment on this earth, and I felt strongly tempted to offer him the few shillings I had in my pocket. The money was useless to me in prison, but it would serve as buoyant air to the wings of this human butterfly. What a contrast between our lots! His head was untroubled with thought, he knew nothing of convictions (except legal ones), and sacrifices for principle had probably never entered within the range of his imagination. He chattered away like a garrulous daw, perched upon the step; while we three in the van were just leaving the sunlight of life for the darkness of imprisonment. Our devotion to principle seemed almost folly, and our passion for reforming the world a species of madness. So it must have appeared eighteen centuries ago, when the Prophet of Nazareth stood in the hall of a palace in Jerusalem. The men and damsels who warmed themselves at the fire must have marvelled at the infatuation of Jesus as he courted the shadow of death.

When "Black Maria" disgorged her breakfast, we were ushered into the great hall of Holloway prison. The Deputy-Governor at once accosted us, and told us to wait, standing against the wall, until he could "see about us." Forgetting the rules and regulations, we resumed our conversation, until we attracted the attention of an underling, who marched up with a lordly air and sternly ordered us to stop talking. Presently two figures leisurely descended the flight of stone steps leading to the offices and the interior of the prison. I recognised one of these as the Governor of Newgate. He had evidently come to introduce us. His companion was Colonel Milman, the Governor of Holloway. After a few minutes' conversation, of which I inferred from their looks that we were the object, they parted, and Colonel Milman then advanced towards us with a genial smile. He busied himself about us in the most hospitable manner, as though we were ornaments to the establishment. Interrogating us as to our occupations, he found that only Mr. Ramsey was acquainted with any mechanical work. In his younger days he had practised the noble art of St. Crispin, but he found that no shoes were made in the place, and he had little taste for cobbling. Relying on some information he had received in Newgate, he inquired, with an air of childlike sincerity, whether there was not some work to do in the Governor's garden. Colonel Milman smiled expressively as he answered that he was "afraid not."

The gallant Governor then went into an office, and as I wanted to speak to him before we were marched off, I walked in after him. "Hi!" exclaimed the officious underling, "you mustn't go in there." But I went in, nevertheless, followed by the fussy officer, who was quietly told by the Governor that he "needn't trouble." I explained to Colonel Milman that my position was peculiar. "Yes," he said, "I know; I saw you at the Old Bailey yesterday," and his look expressed the rest. I then stated that, as there was no Court of Criminal Appeal, I wished to make representations to the Home Office as to the character our trial and the almost unprecedented nature of our sentence; in particular, I wished the Home Secretary to say whether he would sanction our being classed with common thieves for a press offence. I was told that I could have an official form for this purpose; and, thanking the Governor, I withdrew to join my companions.

Let me here thank Colonel Milman for his unvarying kindness. During the whole of my imprisonment he never once addressed me in any other way than he would have addressed me outside; and although he had to carry out a harsh sentence, it was obvious that he shrank from the duty. But this eulogium is too personal. I hasten, therefore, to say that I never heard Colonel Milman speak harshly to a prisoner, or saw a forbidding look on his fine face. One of nature's gentlemen, he could hardly be uncivil to the lowest of the low.

Colonel Milman always dressed well, and the little color he always affected was in harmony with his exuberant figure. It was refreshing to see him occasionally in one's weariness of the dingy prison. He usually stood at the wing-gate as the men filed in from exercise, and answered their salutes, with a word for this one and a smile for that. One day I heard a handsome eulogy on him by a prisoner. He was standing in the open air outside the gate. It was a pleasant summer morning, and he was radiantly happy. A man behind me was evidently struck by the Governor's appearance, for I heard him mutter to his neighbor, "Good old boy, ain't he?" "Yes," said the other, "you're right." "Fat, ain't he?" rejoined number one. "Yes," said number two, "like a top. It do yer good to see somebody as ain't thin."

From the great hall of Holloway prison we were conducted through a passage under the staircase to the basement of the reception wing. Our pockets were emptied, but not searched, and every article stowed away in a little bag. One by one we went into an office, where a clerkly official wrote our descriptions in a book. "What religion?" he inquired, when he came to the theological department. "None," I replied. "What!" he rejoined, "surely you're Catholic or Protestant or something." Then, with a flourish of the pen, and an air of finality, he put the question again more decisively, "What religion?" "None," I said. He stared, gave me up as a bad job, and wrote down "Religion none." That extremely succinct description figured for twelve months on the card outside my cell door, and I have heard prisoners speculating as to what sort of religion "none" was. It was the name of a sect they had never heard of.

The prisoners' cards, affixed to their cell doors, and containing their name, age, crime, sentence, class and creed, were of two colors—white (the emblem of purity) for the Protestants, and red (the symbol of sin) for the Catholics. These criminal members of the two great divisions of Christendom, like their better or more fortunate co-religionists out of doors, do not mix in their devotions. They worship God at different times, although, alas! the same building has to serve for both. No special color has been found requisite for Freethinkers, who seldom trouble the prison officials, although this fact is only another proof of their uncommon obstinacy; for it is clear that, according to their principles, they ought to fill our gaols, yet they perversely refrain from those crimes which every principle of consistency obliges them to commit.

After this ceremony we were conducted upstairs to our cells in the reception wing, to await an opportunity of washing and changing our clothes. We passed several prisoners at work in the corridors. All were silent and stolid, and I could hardly resist the impression that I was in a lunatic asylum. We were handed over to a red-haired and red-bearded warder, who locked us up in separate cells. Before closing my door, he asked whether I was a German, and had any connection with Herr Most. I explained that the Freiheit and the Freethinker were very different papers. "What's your sentence?" he said. "Twelve months." "Whew! but it's a long time." Yes, my red-headed friend, you were quite right. It was indeed a long time!

CHAPTER XI

HOLLOWAY GAOL

A few minutes afterwards the red-haired warder returned with what he called "some dinner." It consisted of a little brown loaf, two or three coarse potatoes, and a dirty-looking tin of pea-soup. I was hungry, but I could not tackle this food. From my earliest childhood I have always had a physical antipathy to pea-soup. The very sight of it raises my gorge. Nor have I any special relish for potatoes, unless they are of good quality and well cooked. I therefore munched the brown bread, and washed it down with cold water. It was a Spartan meal, but a very indigestible one, as I can certify from painful experience. Why a prisoner's stomach should be so grossly abused by a sudden change of diet passes my comprehension. Surely it would not be difficult to introduce the prison fare gradually. There is real danger in a shock to the basic organ of life when all the other organs are painfully accommodating themselves to a radical change of environment. Weak men are sometimes shattered by it. Those who talk about the healthiness of prisons (a subject on which I shall have something to say by-and-bye) would be astonished at the quantity of physic dispensed by the doctor. My constitution is a strong one, and a dyspeptic old friend used to envy my "treble-distilled gastric juice." Before I went to Holloway Gaol I scarcely knew, except inferentially, that I had a stomach; and while I was there I scarcely knew I had anything else.

After dining I walked up and down my cell—tramp, tramp, tramp. How the time crawled, weary hour on hour, like a slow serpent over desert sands. There was nothing to read, nothing to do, nothing to hear, and nothing to see. I was steeped in nothing. And as the senses were unexercised, thought worked on memory till the brain seemed gnawing itself, as a shipwrecked man might assuage his thirst at his own veins. Then imagination, the magician, lovely in weal but terrible in woe, began to weave his spell, and visions arose of dear loved ones agonising beyond the prison walls, to whom my heart yearned through the dividing space with an intense passion that seemed as though its potency might almost annihilate our barriers. Alas! hearts yearn in vain. Nothing avails but strength, and what we cannot achieve the Fates never bestow. My cell walls stood cold and impassable around me, like sentinels of destiny, too vigilant for evasion and too strong for resistance. Brute force overmatches even genius and divinity in the ultimate appeal. Prometheus lies chained to his Caucasian rock, in eternal pain though in eternal defiance; and Napoleon frets away his mighty life at St. Helena watched by the callous eyes of Sir Hudson Lowe.

About three o'clock my cell door was again unlocked and I was invited to take a bath. In the corridor I met my two fellow prisoners, and we were all three marched back to the reception room. Three good baths of warm water were awaiting us. What a glorious luxury after the six days' confinement, without any means of washing one's skin! Some of the prisoners, I understand, regard the first bath as the worst part of the punishment. They are brought up in dirt, and love it; like the Italian who deserted the English girl he was engaged to, and justified himself by saying: "Oh, if I marry her, she wash me, and then I die." We, however, splashed about in our baths, uttering ejaculations of pleasure, and congratulating each other on at least one pleasant bit of prison experience.

The doors of our bath-rooms were about five feet high, with an open space of nine or ten inches between the bottom and the floor. Over the top of these an officer passed us each a couple of shirts (under and over), a pair of drawers, a pair of trousers, and worsted stockings. The drawers and the under-shirt were woollen, and the outer-shirt coarse striped cotton. The trousers seemed a mixture of cotton and wool. They are brown when new, but they wash white, and look then very much like canvas. My pair was a terrible misfit, and had to be exchanged for another nearly twice the size. We were also provided with a net bag to put our own clothes in. My good black suit, dirty linen, hat and boots, were all crushed in together After this performance the bags are hung up, and either the next day, or at their leisure, the officials make an inventory of the contents, and stow them away until the day before the prisoner leaves, when they are taken out in readiness for donning on the blessed morning of release.

Clad in shirt, trousers and stockings, we walked from our baths to the reception room, where we found several officers and the Governor and Deputy-Governor, who had apparently come to superintend our toilet. Each of us was fitted with a new pair of shoes, a waistcoat and a coat. These arrangements were the subject of a good deal of pleasantry. Our garments were not of a Bond Street pattern; indeed, it takes a very handsome man to cut an elegant figure in a prison suit. I maliciously remarked to Mr. Ramsey that he looked like a gentleman out yachting; but somehow he was unable to see himself in that light. My own clothes were sadly defective. The biggest shirt-collar they had would not button round my throat, and the longest stock was so inadequate that a special one had to be made for me. Nor would the biggest coat fasten across my chest. A broad expanse of waistcoat yawned between the button and the button-hole. Fancying that my complaint was merely fractious, the Deputy-Governor—a tall, powerful man—tried to pull them together, and miserably failed. "Well," he said, "it's the largest in stock, and we can't give you what we haven't got." "Yes," I exclaimed, "that's all very well; but if I go about with an open throat like this I shall get an attack of bronchitis. Pray let me have a stock as soon as possible. And do you really mean that you can't possibly find me a bigger coat?" The Deputy-Governor eyed me smilingly as he said, "Come, Mr. Foote, don't be so particular; the clothes don't quite fit you now, but they will." And the worst of it was they did. My coat, however, was always tight across the chest. I changed my trousers and waistcoat as I grew slimmer, but the solid structure of my back and chest (built up by athletics in youth and sustained by lecturing in manhood) always taxed the resources of the establishment in the matter of coats.

One by one we went into the booking-clerk's office again, where we were scaled and our weights entered in a book. Then we had an interview with the doctor, whose duty it was to examine us to see whether we were suffering from any complaint. I was pronounced quite sound. Dr. Gordon spoke pleasantly then, as he always did afterwards. "I suppose you've lived pretty well?" he said. "Not epicureanly," I answered, "but still well." "I'm afraid you won't like our hospitality," he rejoined. "I suppose not," I replied grimly. "However," he continued, "I shall put you on third-class diet at once, and order you a mattress." What the third-class diet was the reader shall learn presently. The second-class diet, which I should otherwise have had for the first month, consists of nothing but bread and sloppy meal-and-water, three times a day. Mr. Kemp had to put up with this wretched fare for a while, and he tells me he was ravenously hungry morning and night, so that it was a luxury to pick up a chance piece of bread from a dinner-tin in the corridor or from a friendly prisoner "off his feed."

Bathing, clothing, and doctoring over, we were marched back to our cells, each loaded with a new mattress and a pair of clean sheets. A few minutes later I was summoned to the schoolroom with Mr. Ramsey, where we were furnished with pen and ink and a sheet of foolscap to write our "petition" to the Home Secretary. The schoolmaster officiated on this occasion. He was a tall, pleasant-looking man, something over forty, with a tendency to baldness. I believe he instructs prisoners who cannot read or write in those useful arts. But his general duty is to play factotum to the chaplain. He takes the singing class, leads the music in chapel, plays the harmonium (the chaplain always calls it the organ), acts as parson's clerk, and reads the lessons when his superior's throat is hoarse with raving. He has a clear and powerful voice, which often serves him in good stead. The congregation has a knack of getting out of time and tune when the melody is unfamiliar; this, in turn, distracts the choir, who flounder hopelessly, until the schoolmaster drags them back by putting full steam on the harmonium and singing at the top of his voice. Every Sunday afternoon, at least, he was obliged to display his vocal prowess in this manner. After every one of the commandments read out by the parson the prisoners chanted the response, "Lord have mercy upon us, and incline our hearts to keep this law." Nine times they chanted thus, gathering momentum as they went along, so that they took the tenth in brave style. But, alas! the tenth was different. "Lord have mercy upon us, and write all these thy laws in our hearts, we beseech thee," were the words, and the tune was correspondingly altered. Fortunately, just at the point of change, there was a strong crescendo, which gave the schoolmaster a fine opportunity of asserting himself. Dragging them back was impossible, so he drowned them, and concluded with the solemn diminuendo amid the breathless admiration of the audience, who went wrong and wondered at his going right every Sunday with the most astonishing regularity.

Looking after the library was the part of the schoolmaster's duty which brought him in frequent contact with me. I always found him very civil and obliging; and from all I could ascertain he was not only generally liked in the prison, but considered a better gentleman than the chaplain.

My "petition" to the Home Secretary was a lengthy document. I assigned many reasons for considering our sentence atrocious. I will not recite them, because they will easily suggest themselves to the readers who have followed my narrative. In conclusion I asked, if our release was impossible, that we might be treated as first-class misdemeanants, according to the general European custom in the case of press offenders, or at least supplied with books and writing materials. Sir William Harcourt sent no answer for a month. At the end of that interval the Governor called me into his office and read out the brutal reply: "The Home Secretary requests Colonel Milman to inform Foote and Ramsey that he sees no reason for acceding to their request."

That was the only instruction Colonel Milman ever received

from the Home Office concerning us. Two months later, when public opinion was more fully aroused in our favor, Sir William Harcourt allowed paragraphs to circulate in the papers, stating that orders were given for our being granted every indulgence consistent with our safe custody. It was a brazen lie, which we were prevented from contradicting by the prison rules. So carefully is every regulation contrived for shielding officials that a prisoner is not allowed, in his quarterly letter, to give any particulars of his treatment. Sir William Harcourt also permitted the newspapers to announce that our health would not be allowed to suffer. Another lie! When, after six weeks' incessant diarrhoea, I complained that my stomach would not accommodate itself to the prison food, and asked to be shifted to the civil side, where I could provide my own, Sir William Harcourt did not even condescend to reply, although he was duly informed that if Mr. Ramsey and I had been found Guilty at the Court of Queen's Bench, on our third trial, Lord Coleridge would not only have made his sentence concurrent with that of Judge North, but also have removed us from the criminal-wards to the debtors' wing. Nay, more. When Mr. Kemp had to be taken to the hospital, where he was confined to his bed, and so weakened that he had to be assisted to the carriage on the morning of his release, Sir William Harcourt would not remit a day of his sentence, or take any notice of his representations. It is well that the public should know this, and contrast Sir William Harcourt's treatment of us with his treatment of Mr. Edmund Yates. From the first I had no expectation of release. I told Colonel Milman that Sir William Harcourt was merely a politician, who cared for nothing but keeping in office; and that unless our friends could threaten some Liberal seats, or seriously affect a division in the House of Commons, he would keep us in to please the bigots and the Tories.

Our "petition" to the Home Secretary being finished, we returned to our cells, where tea was served at six o'clock. It consisted of gruel, or, in prison parlance, "skilly," and another little brown loaf. The liquid portion of this repast was too suggestive of bill-stickers' paste to be tempting, so I made a second meal of bread and water.

The red-haired warder gave me a lesson in bed-making before he locked me up for the night. Hammocks had been dispensed with in Holloway ever since Sir Richard Cross groaned in the travail of invention, and produced his masterpiece and monument—the plank bed. Yet so slow is the official mind, that the rings still lingered in some of the cells. The plank bed is constructed of three eight-inch deals, held together laterally by transverse wooden bars, which serve to lift it two or three inches from the floor. At the head there is a raised portion of flat wood, slightly sloping, to serve as a bolster. For the first month (such is Sir Richard Cross's brilliant idea) every prisoner, no matter what his age or his offence, must sleep on this plank bed without a mattress, unless the doctor sees a special reason for ordering him one. During the second month he sleeps on the plank bed three nights a week, and during the third month one night. Sleeps! The very word is a mockery. Scores of prisoners do not sleep, but pass night after night in broken and restless slumber. Fancy a man delicately brought up, as some prisoners are, suddenly pitched on one of these vile inventions. He tosses about hour after hour, and rises in the morning sore and weary. He has no appetite for breakfast, and is low all day. The next night comes with renewed torture, and on the following day he is still worse. He then applies to see the doctor, who gives him a bottle of physic, which forces an appetite for a while. But it is soon powerless against the effects of nervous exhaustion, and before the poor devil can obtain relief, he is sometimes reduced to the most pitiable condition. I have seen robust men in Holloway, by means of this plank bed and other superfluous tortures of our prison system, brought to the very verge of the grave; and I can scarcely control my indignation when I remember that Mr. Truelove, at the age of seventy, was subjected to this atrocious discipline.

The mattresses are stuffed with fibre. They are tolerable at first, but in a few weeks the stuffing runs into lumps, and your mattress gets nearly as hard as the plank. Shaking is no good; I tried it, and found it only shifted the lumps out of the places my body had forced them in, and left me to repose on a series of hillocks. I got my mattress changed once or twice, but ordinary prisoners are seldom so fortunate.

I retired to rest early that first evening in Holloway. The day had been eventful, and I slept heavily. Breakfast the next morning was a second edition of the tea—bread and skilly; and again I refreshed myself with the little loaf and cold water.

Soon after breakfast I was invited to attend chapel. It was a welcome summons, for the cell is so drearily monotonous that any change is agreeable. The corner of the chapel we entered was partitioned off from the rest of the building, and capable of seating twenty or thirty prisoners. Besides ourselves, there were present ten or twelve boys, three or four old men, and two or three persons who looked slightly imbecile. The service was read by the chaplain, whose voice was loud, authoritative, and repellant. Some people would call it gruff. It was certainly the most unpersuasive voice I ever heard. As I listened to its domineering tones I could hardly refrain from laughing, for they elicited an old story from the depths of memory. An aged pauper lay dying, and in the parson's absence the master officiated at the sinner's exit from this world. "Well, Tom," he began, "you've been a dreadful fellow, and I fear you are going to hell." "Oh, sir," said the poor old fellow, "you don't say so." "Yes, Tom," the master rejoined, "I do say so; and you ought to be thankful there's a hell to go to."

After chapel we spent an hour or so in our cells, and were then conducted to the basement of the reception wing, where we met the Governor, who conducted us through several dark passages that led to the foot of a spiral iron staircase. We ascended this, and found ourselves on the ground floor of the criminal side of the prison. Four wings radiated from a common centre, distinguished by the first four letters of the alphabet. I was taken to the first cell in the first wing, Mr. Ramsey to the second cell in the second wing, and Mr. Kemp to the second cell in the third wing; our numbers being A 2, 1—B 2, 2—and C 2, 2. Colonel Milman personally placed me in charge of a warder who has since left the prison, and I believe the service. He was a good, kind-hearted fellow, who never spoke harshly to anybody. Following me into my cell, he took pains to "put me through the ropes." Before leaving he said, "I'm very sorry to see you here, Mr. Foote. I've been reading your case in the papers. It's a great shame. But I'll do my best to make you comfortable while you're with me." And I must say he did.

There were several prisoners standing mute in the corridor outside, and I remarked that they were a pale looking crew. "Yes," said the warder sadly, "confinement tells on a man." Then he gently closed and locked the door, leaving me alone to begin my long ordeal, with the words humming in my ears like the whisper of a fiend—Confinement tells on a man!

CHAPTER XII

PRISON LIFE

When I found myself alone in my permanent cell, I sat down on the little three-legged stool and examined the furniture. There was a flap-table, two feet by one, fixed on the right wall. In the left corner behind the door were three minute quarter-circle shelves, containing a roll of bedding, a wooden salt-cellar, a wooden spoon, and a comb and brush, each about four inches long. In the opposite corner under the window stood the plank bed, and on the floor were three tin utensils—a dust-pan, a water-can, and a nondescript lidded article for baser uses. Fortunately, the urn-shaped abomination I found in the Newgate cells, and have already described, was absent in Holloway. When a prisoner wished to visit the water-closet, he rang his bell, and sooner or later (often later) he was let out. Each wing had two closets in a deep recess, the door shielding the occupant's person from mid-leg to breast. During the night the nondescript lidded article was brought into requisition. When the cell doors were opened at six o'clock in the morning every prisoner put out his "slops," which were emptied by the cleaners. This scavenger's work must be very distasteful, but so anxious are the prisoners to get out of their cells that there are always plenty of candidates for the office. The tins are kept clean by means of brick and whitening, which are passed into the cells every evening in little cotton bags. My dust-pan, at least, was always well polished, for I used it as a mirror to see how I was looking, being naturally anxious to ascertain what visible effect the prison life had upon me. One of the warders put me up to a very useful "wrinkle." By well cleaning the dust-pan with whitening, rubbing it up well with the clean rag until it had a nice surface, and then lightly passing a rag saturated with dubbin over it, you could produce a beautiful polish by a few slight touches of the "finisher." After this artistic process the dust-pan shone like an oriental mirror, and might have served a belle at her toilette.

Every article of furniture has now been described, excepting the stool. It was a miniature tripod, fifteen inches high, with a round top about eight inches in diameter. A more uncomfortable seat could hardly be devised. There was no support for the back, and the legs had to be stretched out at full length. If you bent them you threw your body forward, and ran the risk of contracting round shoulders. Whenever I wanted a little ease, especially after dinner, when a V-shaped body is not conducive to digestion, I used to rest against the upright plank bed, extend my legs luxuriously, and dream of the cigar which was just the one thing required to complete a picture of comfort.

Such was the furniture of my apartment in Her Majesty's Holloway Hotel. Scantier appointments were impossible. Yet, to my surprise, an officer came in one day with an inventory, to see if anything was missing. Rather a superfluous check, when the iron cell door was constantly locked and there was no opening to the window! A prisoner could hardly bury his furniture in a concrete floor, and the most ferocious appetite would surely quail before deal planks and tin pans.

The cell itself was similar to the one I have already described. The ventilation was provided by an iron grating over the door, communicating with a shaft that carried off the foul air; and another iron grating under the window, which admitted the fresh air from outside. This grating, however, did not communicate directly with the atmosphere, for the prison is built with double walls. Eighteen inches or so below it was another grating in the outer wall. This arrangement prevented the prisoners from getting a glimpse of the grounds, as well as the air from rushing in too rawly. My cell was one of the old ones. In the new cells there is a slightly different method of ventilation. Two of the small panes of glass are removed from the window, and a little frame is placed inside, consisting of wood at the sides and fluted glass in the front. Flush with the window-sill at the bottom, it inclines inward at an angle of twenty degrees, so that there is room at the top for a six-inch flap, which works on hinges, and is elevated or lowered by a chain. This is an improvement on the old system, because the fresh air comes in straight, and you can regulate the inflow. But in both cases the fresh air has to ascend, and unless there is a wind blowing you get very little of it on a hot summer day. The ventilation depending entirely on temperature, without being assisted by a draught, if the outside temperature, as is often the case in the summer, happens to be higher than that of your cell, your atmosphere is stagnant, and you live in a tank of foul air. This defect might be partially remedied by leaving the cell doors open when the prisoners are out at exercise or chapel, and, as it were, refilling the tank. But keys are a fetish in prison, and the officials think it quite as necessary to lock up an empty cell as an occupied one.

The cell floor, I have said, was blackleaded and polished. A small fibre brush was supplied for sweeping up the dust, and a tight roll of black cloth for polishing. I used both these at first, but I soon dispensed with the latter. Having a slight cold, I found my expectoration black, a circumstance that slightly alarmed me until I reflected that my lungs were in excellent order, and that the discoloration must be due to some extrinsic cause. This I discovered to be the blacklead from the floor. It wears off under your tread, and as there is no draught to carry the dust away, it floats in the air and is inhaled. The only remedy was to avoid the blacklead altogether. When, therefore, the bucket containing a quantity in solution was next brought round, I declined to have any. "But you must," said the officer. "Well, I object," I answered, "and I certainly shall not put it on. If you like to do it yourself of course I cannot prevent you." He did not like to do it himself and disappeared, saying he would come again directly, which he forgot to do. Several days afterwards the Deputy-Governor came on a tour of inspection. Noticing that my floor was neither black nor polished, he attempted a mild reproof. I repeated my objection. "Well, you know," he replied, "you must keep your cell clean." "Yes," I rejoined, "and I do keep it clean for my own sake; but your blacklead is dirt." That ended the conversation, and the blacklead question was never agitated again, although once or twice, during my absence from the cell, the obnoxious stuff was put on the floor and polished up by one of the cleaners. Let me add that in the new cells the floors are all boarded, and the blacklead nuisance is there unknown.

While I was meditating on my luxurious surroundings, the warder entered again with a prisoner, who carried a bag. "Well, Mr. Foote," said the genial officer, "how are you getting on? I've brought you some work. It isn't hard, and you needn't task yourself; you'll find it help to pass away the time." Some of the contents of the bag were then emptied on the floor. They consisted of fibre-rope clipped into short lengths. These had to be picked abroad. The work was light, but very monotonous. It did help to kill time, and it was less troublesome than picking oakum. Mr. Truelove tells me that they made him pick oakum in prison till his fingers were raw, and laughed at him for complaining. He was then seventy years old! Think of it, reader, and reflect on the tender mercies of the religion of charity.

During my imprisonment I never worked at anything but fibre-picking. Gladly would I have wheeled a barrow in the open air, but that is a privilege reserved for felons; misdemeanants are locked up in their cells night and day. Once there was an attempt made to instruct me in the art of brush-making, but it egregiously failed. An officer from the D wing, where the mats and brushes are made, opened my cell door one afternoon, and shouted, "Come along!" "Where?" I asked, not liking his manner. "Where!" he ejaculated, "Come along." "Thank you," I said, "but you must please tell me where." He was very much annoyed by my freezing civility, which I always found the best represser of impertinence; but recognising his mistake, he changed his tone, and vouchsafed an explanation. "The Governor," he said, "wants you to come and see how brushes are made." "Oh, of course," I said, and marched after him.

Arriving at the D wing, I was silently introduced to a prisoner sitting on a stool, who had been brought out of his cell to give me lessons in brush-making. He worked and I watched. Presently the officer had to attend to some other business a few yards off. Directly his back was turned the prisoner eagerly whispered, "How long are ye doin'?" I told him. "I'm doin' fifteen months," he confidingly said. Then he added, with look half positive and half interrogative, "Time's damned long, ain't it?" I agreed. Forgetting his work, he spliced a bit of rope badly. "See," I said, "that splice is wrong." "Ah," he replied, his face brightening, "you're a salt un too, are ye? Hanged if I didn't think you was a barnacle." He informed me that he had been in the English and American navies, and all round the world. Where had I been? I was obliged to explain that I was a journalist. Quill-driving, as he called it, was evidently, in his opinion, an ignominious employment. However did I learn splicing! When I explained that I was bred at the seaside, and passionately loved boating, his sailor's heart warmed towards me again. "This work ain't hard," he said; "you can make two brushes in an hour and a half, and I makes a dozen a week." I smiled. It was a fine illustration of what is called prison labor. Resuming, he said: "I'm the only one as makes 'em now, and I s'pose they wants more. The chap as made 'em afore me used to do three dozen a week. Wasn't he a darned fool? Now, don't you go makin' more than two a day, or you'll put my nose out of joint." "No," I promised, "I won't make more than two a day." "Ah," he said, looking at me with a comical twinkle of the eyes, "I see you ain't a goin' to make brushes."

At this point the warder stepped up, and invited me to try my hand. "Thank you," I replied; "the Governor told you to let me see how brushes are made, and I have seen how brushes are made." Then bowing slightly, I walked straight back to my cell, leaving the officer almost petrified with astonishment. I heard no more of brush-making.

My objection to the work was simple. It was more interesting than picking fibre, but it necessitated stooping, the brush being held, like a shoe, between the knees. As a lecturer, I knew too well the value of a sound chest to engage in such employment.

I come now to the diet. Third-class fare, to which I was entitled by the doctor's order, was almost entirely farinaceous, and miserably monotonous. Breakfast and tea (or supper), served at eight and six respectively, consisted of six ounces of brown bread and three quarters of a pint of gruel, or "skilly." The latter was frequently so fluid that spooning was unnecessary. The dinners, served punctually at twelve o'clock, were more varied. Brown bread and browner potatoes were the staple of each mid-day meal. The bread was always excellent. The potatoes were abominable. I have said that they were browner than the bread, and I may add that the color was not caused by cooking, but purely original. As the old potatoes were leaving the market, and the new ones were too expensive for prisoners, the most robust appetite must have turned with disgust from the supply which fell to our share. I should imagine that every swine's trough around the metropolis must have been plundered to provision Holloway Gaol.

The variable part of the dinner was as follows. Pea-soup, to which, as I have already said, I had a physical antipathy, was served up three days out of every seven—on Tuesdays, Thursdays, and Saturdays. And such pea-soup! The mixture used to rise as I swallowed it, and I have often grasped my throat to keep it down, knowing that if I did not eat, however nauseous the food, my health would necessarily suffer. It was not pea-soup before the joint, but pea-soup without it, and in that case the quality of the compound is an important matter. When I read the Book of Job afresh in my cell, I found in the sixth chapter, and seventh verse, a text which admirably suited my situation: "The things that my soul refused to touch are as my sorrowful meat." Three days a week I could have preached a better, or at least a more feeling, sermon on that text than any parson in the kingdom.

On Sundays and Wednesdays, instead of the pea-soup, I was served with six ounces of suet pudding baked in a separate tin. I never saw such pudding, and I never smelt such suet. Brown meal was used for the dough, and the suet lay on the top in yellow greasy streaks. I can liken the compound to nothing but a linseed poultice. The resemblance was so obvious that it struck many other prisoners. I have heard the term poultice applied to the suet pudding more than once in casual conversations in the exercise ground. Twice a week I was entitled to meat. On Friday, instead of the pea-soup or suet pudding, there was three ounces of Australian beef; and on Mondays three-quarters of an ounce of fat bacon with some white beans. The subtle humorist who drew up the diet scale had appended a note that "all meats were to be weighed without bone."

A good tale hangs by that bacon and beans. While I was awaiting the second trial in Newgate, and providing my own food, I studied the diet scale which hangs up in each cell, and was fascinated by this extravagant quantity of pork, which seemed to evidence an unimagined display of prison hospitality. One of the officers to whom I mentioned the matter said, "Ah, Mr. Foote, I wish you would show that diet up when you get out. Untried prisoners have the same fare as condemned criminals, only they get less of it. There are lusty chaps come in here, some of them quite innocent, who could eat twice as much, and look round for the man that cooked it. I'll tell you a story about that three-quarters of an ounce. A fellow rang his bell one day after the dinner was served. 'Well,' I said, 'what's the matter?' 'I want's my bacon,' said he. 'Well, you've got it,' said I. 'No I aint,' said he. 'It's in your tin,' said I. 'Taint in my tin,' said he. Then I fetched up the cook. We all three searched, and at last we found the bacon in one of the shucks of the beans."

The worthy fellow laughed, and so did I, as he ended his story. There might have been some exaggeration in it, but you would not find it so hard to believe if you had ever sat down to dine on three-quarters of an ounce of fat bacon.

I was confined in my cell twenty-three hours out of every twenty-four, and during the first week my one hour's exercise was mostly taken in the corridor instead of in the open air. The prison authorities are careless about a man's health being subtly undermined, but they do not like him to catch cold, which may produce visible and audible consequences. Whenever it is snowing or raining, or whenever the ground is wet, the prisoners exercise in the corridors, where the air is scarcely purer than in their cells. During the first week, the weather being bad, I only went out once. On Saturday, which was cleaning day, I had no exercise at all, and on Sunday I was entitled to none—prisoners not being allowed that privilege on the blessed Sabbath until a month of their sentence has expired. I was therefore confined to my cell without exercise or fresh air from Friday morning until Monday morning, or three clear days. The exercise out of doors is a delightful relief from solitary confinement in a brick vault. The prisoners walk in Indian file in circles: a regular thieves' procession, the Rogue's March without the music. The new comers, who violate the rule of silence, are soon detected by the vigilant officers, but the old hands, as I have said, acquire a habit of speaking without moving the lips, and in a tone which just reaches their next neighbor. Ten days or so after I entered Holloway I overheard the following conversation behind me:—

"Who's that bloke in front o' you?" "Dunno," was the reply. "Queer lookin' bloke, aint he?"—"How long's he doin'?"—"A stretch," which in prison language means twelve months, and having served that term, I know that it is a stretch. "What's he in for?"—"Dunno, but I hear he put somethin' in a paper they didn't like."—"What, a stretch for that!"—And I venture to assert that, although the prisoner who uttered this ejaculation was on the wrong side of a gaol, his unsophisticated common sense on this point was infinitely superior to the bigotry of Giffard, Harcourt, and North, and of the jury who assisted in sending us to gaol for "putting something in a paper they didn't like."

During my first week's residence in Holloway Gaol, owing to the bad weather, I exercised in the corridor with the other inmates of the A wing. There is little more room between the cell doors and the railing overlooking the well than suffices for the passage of a single person. The prisoners therefore walked in Indian file, and as they were practically beyond supervision except when they came abreast of one of the three or four officers in charge, a great deal of conversation went on, and I wondered why the chief warder below did not hear the loud hum of so many voices. I afterwards discovered the reason. When you stand under the procession you can hear nothing but the trampling of dozens of feet, which reverberates through the wing, and drowns every other sound.

At first I marched as stiff as a poker, drawing myself together, as it were, into the smallest compass, to avoid the contamination of the company, most of whom were poor, repulsive specimens of humanity, survivals in our civilised age of the lower types of barbarous or savage times. Most of them were young and had a reckless bearing, but a few were middle-aged, and some were obviously old hands who "knew the ropes," were reconciled to their fate, and resolved on making the best of the situation. Tramp, tramp, tramp! My very life seemed reduced to this monotonous shuffle. I half fancied myself in a new kind of hell, ranked in an everlasting procession of aimless feet, mechanically following a convict's coat in front of me, and as mechanically followed by the wearer of a similar coat behind. But as I passed the great window at the end of the wing the blessed light of the silvery winter sun sometimes streamed through the dense glass upon my face, rays of the eternal splendor coming so many millions of miles from the great fire-fount, how indifferent, as Perdita saw, to the artificial distinctions of men! I felt refreshed, but the feeling wore off as I returned to the gloomy corridor, skirting cells on the right, and on the left a low rail that offered the suicide a tempting leap into the arms of Death. All this time I was living an intense inward life, but I suppose there was a far-away look in my eyes, for now and then a prisoner would say "Cheer up, sir." I smiled at this consolatory effort, for although I was disgusted, I was not despondent. Occasionally an attempt was made to drag me into conversation, but I parried all advances with as little offence as possible. One dirty short man, grievously afflicted with scurvy, or something worse, several times manoeuvred to get behind me, and at last he succeeded. "How long ye doin', mate?" No answer. "I say, mate, how long ye doin'?" No answer. "A damned long time, I know, or they wouldn' give ye a —— new suit like that, ye stuck-up ———."

What oaths I heard in that wretched gaol! No abomination of human speech is unknown to me. One particularly vile expletive was fashionable during my imprisonment; it seasoned every phrase, and preceded every adjective. Its constant iteration was sickening, until long experience made me callous. How thankful I should be to Judge North for trying to purify me in that mud-bath of rascality. I can never forget the debt of gratitude—and I never will!

Among the prisoners I noticed one of robust physique and martial bearing. Seldom had I seen so fine a figure. Within six months I saw that man reduced almost to a skeleton by solitary confinement, wearily trailing one limb after the other, and looking out despairingly from cavernous, moribund eyes. Well did Lord Fitzgerald (I think) in a recent speech in the House of Lords describe this torture as the worst ever devised by the brain of man. His lordship added that the Governor of a great prison told him that he never knew a man undergo twelve months of such punishment without severe suffering, or two years of it without being terribly shaken, or three years without being physically and mentally wrecked. In the penal servitude establishments the discipline has to be relaxed, or the prisoners would die or go mad before their terms expired. They work out of their cells in the daytime, and on certain occasions (Sundays, I believe) they are allowed to walk in couples and exercise their faculty of speech.

The poor fellow I refer to, fearing that he would die, and having learnt that I was a public man, managed to tell me something of his case. He had been a warder in Coldbath Fields Prison, where he officiated as master-tailor. In an evil moment he "cabbaged" some cloth, was detected, tried, condemned, and sentenced to twenty months' imprisonment. He had been in the army for over twenty years without a scratch of the pen against his name, and his officers had given him excellent characters; but the judge would hear of nothing in mitigation of sentence, although he knew it deprived the man of a pension of thirty-six pounds a year, which he had earned by long service in India, where the enemy's blades had drunk deeply of his blood. His wife and children had gone to a work-house in Leicestershire, and as they had no money for travelling, he had never received a visit. He pined away in his miserable cell until he became a pitiable spectacle which excited the compassion of the whole prison. The doctor ordered him out of his cell, but the authorities would not allow it. He told me how much he had lost round the chest and calf, but I have forgotten the precise figures. One fact, however, I recollect distinctly; he had lost eight inches round the thigh, and his flesh was like a child's. Eventually the doctor peremptorily ordered him into the hospital, and the Prison Commissioners and Visiting Magistrates were reluctantly obliged to let him save the man's life.

Dreary indeed was the life in my prison cell, sitting on the three-legged stool picking fibre, or walking up and down the twelve-foot floor. I used frequently to stand under the window for long intervals, resting my hand on the sloping sill. It was impossible to see through the heavy-fluted panes, but outside was light, liberty and life. Sometimes, especially on Saturdays, when I had been accustomed to run down to the North, the Midlands or the West, to fulfil a lecturing engagement, the muffled shriek of a distant railway whistle went through me like the clash of steel.

My library, during the first three months, consisted of a Bible, a Prayer Book and a Hymn Book. Although I was really there for knowing too much about the "blessed book" already, I read it right through in the first month, and again in the second, besides reading it discursively afterwards. And still, I am a sincerely impenitent Freethinker! You may knock a man down with the Bible, and make an impression on his skull; but when he picks himself up again, you find you have made no impression on his mind, except that his opinion of you is altered. I remember the chaplain calling to see me one day as I was just concluding my inspection of what Heine calls the menagerie of the Apocalypse. He could not help seeing the Bible, for when it lay open there was very little table visible. "Ah," he said, "I see you have been reading the holy Scripture." "Yes," I replied, "I've read it through this month, and I believe I'm the only man in the place who has done it—including the chaplain."

By and by the schoolmaster hunted me out a French Bible, the only one in the prison. It was an old one, and contained some scratches by a Gallic prisoner, who had been twice immured for smuggling (pour contrabandier), and who pathetically called on God to help him. Cette vie est vie amere, he had written. Yes, my poor French friend, it was bitter indeed! As for the hymn book, it contained two or three good pieces, like Newman's "Lead, Kindly Light," but for the rest it was the scraggiest collection I ever met with—evangelical and wooden, with an occasional dash of weak music and washy sentiment.

The monotony of my existence was not even broken by visits to chapel. After the first day's attendance at "divine worship" for some reason I was not let out at the hour of devotion. After a few days, however, one of the principal officers said to me "Wouldn't you like to go to chapel, Mr. Foote. There's nothing irksome in it, and you'll find it breaks the monotony." "With pleasure," I replied, "but I have not till now received an invitation." "What!" he exclaimed. Then, calling up a young Irish officer in my wing, he asked "How is this? Why hasn't Mr. Foote been invited to chapel?" "Well, sir," answered the culprit, scratching his head and looking sheepish, "I knew Mr. Foote was a Freethinker, and I didn't want to insult his opinions." Good! I thought. Why was not this worthy fellow on the jury, or better still, on the bench? I told him I was very much obliged for his intended kindness, but at the same time I preferred going to chapel, as I wished to see all I could for my money. After that I went to the house of prayer like any church-going belle (this is what Cowper must have meant, for how could a bell go to church?) every Sunday, and every other day during the week. Had the chapel been of larger dimensions I should have gone daily, but it was too small to hold all the prisoners, who were therefore divided into two congregations, each approaching the holy altar on alternate days. What I saw and heard in the sacred edifice will be related in a separate chapter.

At the end of my second month I was entitled to a school-book and a slate and pencil. These articles were promptly brought to me by the obliging school-master. Two copies of Colenso's Arithmetic had been procured; one was given to me, and the other, as I afterwards learned, to Mr. Ramsey. The fly-leaf was cut out, I noticed; the object being to prevent us from obtaining a bit of paper to write on. This, I may add, is the general rule in the prison library, every book being thus mutilated. It is a silly precaution, for if a prisoner can succeed in carrying on a correspondence with his friends outside, he is obviously not dependent on the library for materials, and he would be the veriest fool to excite suspicion by amputating the leaves of a book.

Knowing that I should have no better school-book during my long imprisonment, I determined to make Colenso last as long as possible. I steadily went through it from beginning to end. Working the addition and subtraction sums was certainly tedious, but I wanted to keep the interesting problems, as you reserve the daintier portions of a repast, till the end. Curiously enough, it was the sober and serious Colenso who gave me my one restless night in Holloway Gaol. I puzzled over one pretty problem, and the bed-bell rang before I could solve it. Directly my gas was turned out the method of solution flashed on my mind, and I was so vexed at being unable to work it out immediately that it was hours before I could fall asleep. During that time my brain made desperate but futile efforts to reach the answer by mental arithmetic, and when I woke in the morning I felt thoroughly fagged.

Having had no writing materials for two months the slate and pencil looked very inviting. I composed a few pieces of verse, including a sonnet on Giordano Bruno and some epigrams on Parson Plaford, Judge North, Sir Hardinge Giffard, and other distasteful personages. But as every piece written on the slate had to be rubbed out to make room for the next, I soon sickened of composition. It was murdering one bantling to make place for another.

Sometimes the dulness of my incarceration was relieved by overhearing whispered conversations outside my cell door. Until we became well known, there was considerable speculation among the prisoners as to who we were, and what we were there for. One day a couple of fellows, engaged in cleaning the corridor, worked themselves near together, one standing on either side of my door. "Who's the bloke in yer?" I heard queried. "Dunno," said the other, "I b'lieve he's a Fenian." Another time I heard the answer, "Oh, he's one of Bradlaugh's pals; and Bradlaugh's coming up next week"—a next week which happily never arrived.

Mr. Ramsey tells me that similar speculations went on outside his door. Like mine, his card specified "misdr." (misdemeanor) as the offence, the officials perhaps not liking to write blasphemy. Like me also, he was put down as a Fenian. "Why there," said a prisoner, who had just enounced this opinion, "look at his card; see— murder!" The "misdr." was not written too plainly, and "murder" was his interpretation of the hieroglyph.

Let me here interpolate another good story in connexion with Mr. Ramsey. He was confidently asked by an old hand what he was in for. "Blasphemy," said Mr. Ramsey. "Blasphemy! What the hell's that?" said the fellow. Here was a confirmed criminal who had never heard of this crime before; it was not in the catalogue known to his fraternity; and on learning that all which could be got from it was nine months' imprisonment if you were found out, and nothing if you were not, he concluded that he would never patronize that line of business.

From the description already given of my cell, the reader has seen that my domestic accommodations were exceedingly limited. All my ablutions were performed with the aid of a tin bowl, holding about a quart. This sufficed for hands and face, but how was I to get a wash all over? I broached this question one day to warder Smith, who informed me that the bathing appliances of the establishment were scanty, and that the prisoners were only "tubbed" once a fortnight. I explained to him that I was not used to such uncleanliness; but of course he could not help me. Then I laid the matter before the Deputy-Governor, who told an officer to take me to the bath-room at the base of the debtor's wing, where I enjoyed a good scrub. On returning to the criminal part of the prison I had my hair cut, a prisoner officiating as barber. Despite the rule of silence, I gave him verbal instructions how to proceed, otherwise he would have given me the regular prison crop. During the rest of my term I always had my hair trimmed in my own fashion. The prison crop, I may observe, is rather a custom than a rule; the regulations require only such hair-cutting and shaving as is necessary for health and cleanliness, but the criminal population affect short hair, and the difficulty is not to bring them under, but to keep them out of, the barber's hands.

Prison barbers are generally amateurs. Of course the officers are above such work, and unless a member of the tonsorial profession happens to be in residence, the scissors are wielded by the first man who fancies himself a natural adept at the business. The last barber I saw in Holloway Gaol was a coachman, whose only qualification for the work was that he had clipped horses' legs. He wore a blue apron round a corpulent waist, and looked remarkably like a pork-butcher. He walked round the victim like an artist engaged on a bust, and his habit was to work steadily away at one spot until the skin showed like a piece of white plaster, after which he labored at another spot, and so on, until the task was finished. Seeing on my head an uncommon mass of hair, he made many desperate solicitations to be allowed an opportunity of displaying his skill, but I steadily resisted the appeal, although it evidently cut him to the quick.

The bathing-house for the criminal prisoners has eight compartments. In the ordinary course, I should have formed one of a detachment of that number, but an exception was made in my case, and I was always taken to bathe alone. Behind the bath-room were the dark cells. I was allowed to inspect these miserable, black holes. They were damp and fetid, and when the door was closed you were in Egyptian darkness. I cannot conceive that such horrid punishment is necessary or justifiable. The prison authorities have every inmate absolutely in their power, and if they are obliged to resort to the black-hole, it must be from want of foresight or the general imbecility of the system.

The flogging was always done outside the black-hole, in the bath-room at the foot of the D wing. I have often heard screaming wretches dragged along the corridor, and their cries of agony as their backs were lacerated by the cat. Singularly, the dinner hour was always selected for this performance, which must have been a great stimulus to the appetites of new comers. One man who was lashed told me it was weeks before his flesh healed. I do not believe that the cat and the dark hole are necessary to prison discipline. They brutalise and degrade both prisoners and officials.

The doctor was astonished one morning by my application for a tooth-brush. Such a thing was never seen or heard of in a prison. I was obliged therefore to use my middle finger, which I found a very inefficient substitute. Another difficulty arose on the shirt question. The prisoners are allowed a clean outer shirt every week, and a clean inner shirt every fortnight. I explained that I would prefer the order reversed, but was told that I could not be accommodated. But I persisted. I wearied the upper officials with applications, and finally obtained a clean kit weekly. Even then I found it necessary to badger them still further. The fortnightly intervals between the baths were too long, and at last I got the Governor to let me have a tub of cold water in my cell every night. This luxury of cleanliness was the best feature in the programme, although my fellow-prisoners appeared to regard it as an unaccountable fad.

One or two brief conversations with the Governor were also an agreeable variation. I found him to be a disciple and friend of the late F. D. Maurice, one of whose books he offered to lend me. He was astonished to find that I had read it, as well as other works by the same author, which he had not read. Colonel Milman expressed a good deal of admiration for Mr. George Jacob Holyoake, and he was still more astonished when I told him that this gentleman had occupied a blasphemer's cell in the old stirring days, when he fiercely attacked Christianity instead of flattering it. "Nothing would give me greater pleasure," said the gallant Governor, "than to hear from you some day as a believer." "Sir," I replied, "I would not have you entertain any such hope, for it will never be realised. My Freethought is not a hobby, but a conviction. You must remember that I have been a Christian, that I know all that can be said in defence of your creed, and that I am well acquainted with all your best writers. I am a Freethinker in spite of this; I might say because of it. And can you suppose that my imprisonment will induce me to regard Christianity with a more friendly eye? On the contrary, it confirms my belief that your creed, to which you are personally so superior, is a curse, and carries the spirit of persecution in its heart of hearts."

Colonel Milman smiled sadly. He began to see that the sceptical disease in me was beyond the reach of physic.

CHAPTER XIII

PARSON PLAFORD

The Gospel of Holloway Gaol, with which Judge North essayed my conversion, produced the opposite effect. Parson Plaford, the prison chaplain, was admirably adapted by nature to preach it. I have already referred to his gruff voice. He generally taxed it in his sermon, and I frequently heard his thunderous accents in the depths of my cell, when he was preaching to the other half of the establishment. His personal appearance harmonised with his voice. His countenance was austere, and his manner overbearing. The latter trait may have been intensified by his low stature. It is a fact of general observation that there is no pomposity like the pomposity of littleness. Parson Plaford may be five feet four, but I would lay anything he is not five feet five. I will, however, do him the justice of saying that he read the lessons with clearness and good emphasis, and that he strove to prevent his criminal congregation from enjoying the luxury of a stealthy nap. He occasionally furnished them with some amusement by attempting to lead the singing. The melody of his voice, which suggested the croak of an asthmatical raven, threw them into transports of sinister appreciation; and the remarkable manner in which he sometimes displayed the graces of Christian courtesy to the schoolmaster afforded them an opportunity of contrasting the chaplain with the Governor.

Parson Plaford's deity was an almighty gaoler. The reverend gentlemen took a prison view of everything. He had a habit, as I learned, of asking new comers what was their sentence, and informing them that it ought to have been twice as long. In his opinion, God had providentially sent them there to be converted from sin by the power of his ministry. I cannot say, however, that the divine experiment was attended with much success. The chaplain frequently told us from the pulpit that he had some very promising cases in the prison, but we never heard that any of them ripened to maturity. When he informed us of these hopeful apprentices to conversion, I noticed that the prisoners near me eyed him as I fancy the Spanish gypsies eyed George Borrow when they heard him read the Bible. Their silence was respectful, but there was an eloquent criticism in their squint.

After one of his frequent absences in search of health, Parson Plaford related with great gusto a real case of conversion. On one particular morning a prisoner was released, who expressed sincere repentance for his sins, and the chaplain's locum tenens had written in the discharge book that he believed it was "a real case of conversion to God." That very morning, I found by comparing notes, also witnessed the release of Mr. Kemp. All the parson-power of Holloway Gaol had failed to shake his Freethought. His conversion would have been a feather in the chaplain's hat, but it could not be accomplished. The utmost that could be achieved was the conversion of a Christian to Christianity.

On another occasion, Parson Plaford ingenuously illustrated the character of prison conversions. An old hand, a well-known criminal who had visited the establishment with wearisome frequency, was near his discharge. He had an interview with the chaplain and begged assistance. "Sir," he said, "I've told you I was converted before, and you helped me. It wasn't true, I know; but I am really converted this time. God knows it sir." But the chaplain would not be imposed upon again. He declined to furnish the man with the assistance he solicited. "And then," said the preacher, with tears in his voice, "he cursed and swore; he called me the vilest names, which I should blush to repeat, and I had to order him out of the room." "Oh," he continued, "it is an ungrateful world. But holy scripture says that in the latter days unthankfulness shall abound, and these things are signs that the end is approaching. Blessed be God, some of us are ready to meet him." These lachrymose utterances were the precursors of a long disquisition on his favorite topic—the end of the world, the grand wind-up of the Lord's business. We were duly initiated into the mysteries of prophecy, a subject which, as South said, either finds a man cracked or leaves him so. The latter days and the last days were accurately distinguished, and it was obscurely hinted that we were within measurable distance of the flaming catastrophe.

Over forty sermons fell from Parson Plaford's lips into my critical ears, and I never detected a grain of sense in any of them. Nor could I gather that he had read any other book than the Bible. Even that he appeared to have read villainously, for he seemed ignorant of much of its contents, and he told us many things that are not in it. He placed a pen in the fingers of the man's hand which disturbed Belshazzar's feast, and gave us many similar additions to holy writ. Yet he was singularly devoid of imagination. He took everything in the Bible literally, even the story of the descent of the Holy Ghost upon the apostles in the shape of cloven tongues of fire.

"They were like this," he said, making an angle with the knuckles of his forefinger on the top of his bald head, and looking at us with a pathetic air of sincerity. It was the most ludicrous spectacle I ever witnessed.

During the few visits he paid me, Parson Plaford was fairly civil. Mr. Ramsey seems to have been the subject of his impertinence. My fellow-prisoner was informed that we deserved transportation for life. Yet at that time the chaplain had not even seen the publication for which we were imprisoned! However, his son had, and he was "a trustworthy young man." Towards the end of his term Mr. Ramsey found the charitable heart of the man of God relent so far as to allow that transportation for life was rather too heavy a punishment for our offence, which only deserved perpetual detention in a lunatic asylum.

For the last ten months of my term Parson Plaford neither honoured nor dishonored my cell with his presence. Soon after I was domiciled in the A wing he called to see me. I rose from my stool and made him a satirical bow. This greeting, however, was too freezing for his effusiveness. Notwithstanding the opinion of us he had expressed to Mr. Ramsey, and with which I was of course unacquainted, he extended his hand as though he had known me for years.

"Ah," he said, "this is a sorry sight. Your trouble is mental I know. I wish I could help you, but I cannot. You are here for breaking the law, you know." "Yes," I replied, "such as it is. But the law is broken every week. Millions of people abstain from attending church on Sunday, yet there is an unrepealed law which commands them to."

"Yes, and I'd make them," was the fiery answer from the little man, as the bigot flamed in his eyes.

"Come now," I said, "you couldn't if you tried."

"Well," he said, "you've got to suffer. But even if you are a martyr, you don't suffer what our martyrs did."

"Perhaps not," I retorted, "but I suffer all your creed is able to inflict. Doesn't it occur to you as strange and monstrous that Christianity, which boasts so of its own martyrs, should in turn persecute all who differ from it? Suppose Freethought had the upper hand, and served you as you serve us: wouldn't you think it shameful?"

"Of course," he blurted. Then, correcting himself, he added: "But you never will get the upper hand."

"How do you know?" I asked. "Freethought has the upper hand in France."

"Yes," he replied, "but that is an infidel country. It will never be so here."

"But suppose," I continued, "it were so here, and we imprisoned you for deriding our opinions as you imprison us for deriding yours. Would you not say you were persecuted?"

"Oh," he said, "that's a different thing."

Mr. Bradlaugh was then mentioned.

"By the way, you're remarkably like him," said the chaplain.

I thought it a brilliant discovery, and still more so when I learned, a few minutes later, that he had not seen Mr. Bradlaugh for thirty years.

Darwin was referred to next.

"I suppose you know he's been disproved," said the chaplain, complacently.

"No, I don't," I answered; "nor do I quite understand what you mean. What has been disproved?"

"Why," he said, "I mean that man isn't a monkey."

"Indeed!" I rejoined; "I am not aware that Darwin ever said that man is a monkey. Nor do I think so myself—except in some extreme cases."

Whether this was construed as a personality or not I am unable to decide, but our interview soon terminated. Parson Plaford called on me two or three times during the next few weeks, promised me some good books to read as soon as the regulations permitted, and fulfilled his promise by never visiting me again.

Mr. Ramsey was nursed a little longer. I suppose the chaplain had hopes of him. But he finally relinquished them when Mr. Ramsey said one Monday morning, on being asked what he thought of yesterday's sermon, "I wonder how you could talk such nonsense. Why, I could preach a better sermon myself."

"Could you?" bristled the little man. And from that moment he gave Mr. Ramsey up for lost.

One day the chaplain ran full butt against Mr. Kemp in the corridor. "Ah," he said, "how are you getting on?" Mr. Kemp made a curt reply. The fact was, he was chewing a small piece of tobacco, an article which does somehow creep into the prison in minute quantities, and is swapped for large pieces of bread. Mr. Kemp was enjoying the luxury, although it would have been nauseous in other circumstances; for the prison fare is so insipid that even a dose of medicine is an agreeable change. Now Parson Plaford and Mr. Kemp are about the same height, and lest the chaplain should see or smell the tobacco, the little blasphemer was obliged to turn his head aside, hoping the conversation would soon end. But the little parson happened to be in a loquacious mood, and the interview was painfully prolonged. Next Sunday there was a withering sermon on "infidels," who were described as miserable persons that "dare not look you in the face."

Parson Plaford seemed to be on very intimate terms with his maker. If his little finger ached, the Lord meant something by it. Yet, although he was always ready to be called home, he was still more ready to accept the doctor's advice to take a holiday when he felt unwell. The last sermon I heard him preach was delivered through a sore throat, a chronic malady which he exasperated by bawling. He told us that the work and worry were too much for him, and the doctor had ordered him rest, if he wished to live. He was going away for a week or two to see what the Lord meant to do with him; and I afterwards heard some of the prisoners wonder what the Lord was doing with him. "I speak to you as a dying man," said the chaplain, as he had said several times before when he felt unwell; and as it might be the last time he would ever preach there, he besought somebody, as a special act of gratitude, to get saved that very day.

One of the prisoners offered a different reason for the chaplain's temporary retirement. "He ain't ill, sir. I knows what 'tis. I was down at the front when your friend Mr. Ramsey went out. There was a lot of coaches and people, and the parson looked as white as a ghost. He thinks ther'll be more coaches and people when you goes out, and he's gone off sooner than see 'em."

During the chaplain's absences his locum tenens was usually a gentleman of very opposite characteristics. He was tall, thin, modest, and even diffident. He slipped into your cell, as I said before, with the deferential air of an undertaker. His speech was extremely soft and rapid, although he stuttered a little now and then from nervousness. "I suppose you know," I asked on his first visit, "what I am here for?" "Y-e-s," he stammered, with something like a blush. I said no more, for it was evident he wished to avoid the subject, and I really think he was sorry to see me persecuted in the name of Christ. He had called, he said, to see whether he could do anything for me. Could he lend me any books? I thanked him for the proffered kindness, but I had my own books to read by that time. Mr. Stubbs's sermons were much superior to Mr. Plaford's. They were almost too good for the congregation. He dwelt with fondness on the tender side of Christ's character, and seemed to look forward to a heaven which would ultimately contain everybody.

On one occasion we had a phenomenal old gentleman in the pulpit. He was white-haired but florid. His appearance was remarkably youthful, and his voice sonorous. I heard that he was assistant chaplain at one of the other London prisons. With the most exemplary fidelity he went through the morning service, omitting nothing; unlike Parson Plaford, who shortened it to leave time for his sermon. I wondered whether he would get through it by dinner-time, or whether he would continue it in the afternoon. But he just managed to secure ten minutes for his sermon, which began with these extraordinary words, that were sung out at the top of his voice: "When the philosopher observes zoophyte formations on the tops of mountains, he," etc. How singularly appropriate it was to the congregation. The sermon was not exactly "Greek" to them, but it was all "zoophyte." I heard some of them wonder when that funny old boy was coming again.

The prisoners sit in chapel on backless benches, tier above tier, from the rails in front of the clerk's desk almost to the roof behind. Two corners are boarded off within the rails, one for the F wing and the other for the debtors' wing. Above them is a long gallery, with private boxes for the governor, the doctor and the chief warder, and a pulpit for the chaplain. Parson Plaford used to make a great noise in closing the heavy door behind the pulpit, leading to the front of the prison; and he rattled the keys as though he loved the sound. He placed them on the desk beside the "sacred volume," and I used to think that the Bible and the keys went well together. In offering his first private prayer, as well as in his last after the benediction, he always covered his face with the sleeve of his robe, lest, I suppose, the glory of his countenance, while communicating with his maker, should afflict us as the insufferable splendor of the face of Moses afflicted the Jews at Mount Sinai. His audible prayers were made kneeling with clasped hands and upturned face. His eyes were closed tightly, his features were painfully contracted, and his voice was a falsetto squeak. I fancy the Governor must have sighed at the performance. The doctor never troubled to attend it.

The prisoners were supposed to cross their hands in front while in chapel. Several unsuccessful attempts were made to induce me to conform to the regulation. I declined to strike prescribed attitudes. Another rule, pretty rigorously enforced, was that the prisoners should look straight before them. If a head was turned aside, an officer bawled out "Look to your front." I once heard the injunction ludicrously interpolated in the service. "Dearly beloved brethren," said the chaplain. "Look to your front," growled the officer. It was text and comment.

Only once did I see a prisoner impressed. The man sat next to me; his face was red, and he stared at the chaplain with a pair of goggle eyes. Surely, I thought, the parson is producing an effect. As we were marching back to our cells I heard a sigh. Turning round, I saw my harvest-moon-faced friend in an ecstacy. It was Sunday morning, and near dinner time. Raising his hands, while his goggle eyes gleamed like wet pebbles, the fellow ejaculated—"Pudden next."

I have already referred to the chapel music, in which the schoolmaster played such a distinguished part. A few more notes on this subject may not be out of place. There was a choir of a dozen or so prisoners, most of whom were long-term men in some position of trust. Short-timers are not, I believe, eligible for membership; indeed, the whole public opinion of the establishment is against these unfortunates, who have committed no crime worth speaking of; and I still remember with what a look of disgust the worthy schoolmaster once described them to me as "Mere parasites, here to-day and gone to-morrow." Having a bit of a voice, I was invited to join the sweet psalmists of Holloway; but I explained that I was only a spectator of the chapel performances, and could not possibly become an assistant. The privileges enjoyed by the choristers are not, however, to be despised. They drop their work two or three times a week for practice, and they have an advantage in matters which are trifling enough outside, but very important in prison. In chapel they sit together on the front benches, and if they smile and whisper they are not so sharply reprimanded as the common herd behind them.

Another privileged class were the cooks, who occupied the last bench, and rested their backs against the wall. They were easily distinguished by their hair being greased, no other prisoners having fat enough to waste on such a luxury.

Saturday morning's chapel hour was devoted to general practice, which was known as the cat's chorus. Imagine three or four hundred prisoners all learning a new tune! Some of the loudest voices were the most unmusical, and the warblers at the rear were generally behind in time as well as in space. How they floundered, gasped, broke down, got up again, and shuffled along as before till the next collapse! Sometimes they gave it up as hopeless, a few first, and then others, until some silly fellow was left shrilling alone, when he too would suddenly stop, as though frightened at the sound of his own voice.

I noticed, however, that whenever an evangelical hymn was sung to an old familiar tune, they all joined in, and rattled through it with great satisfaction. This confirmed the notion I had acquired from previous reading, that nine out of every ten prisoners in our

English gaols have been Sunday-school children, or attendants at church or chapel. Scepticism has not led them to gaol, and religion has not kept them out of it.

Parson Plaford, as I have said, never visited me after the second month. He heard my defence on the third trial before Lord Coleridge, and sadly confessed to Mr. Ramsey that he was afraid I was a hardened sinner. He appears to have had some hopes of my fellow prisoner, whom he continued to visit for another month. Mr. Ramsey encouraged him in doing so, for a conversation with anyone and on anything is a welcome break in the monotony of silence. But when he got books to read there was less need of these interviews, and they soon ceased. Mr. Ramsey informs me, however, that the chaplain called on him just before he left, and asked whether he could offer any suggestions as to the "system." The old gentleman admitted that he had been operating on prisoners for over twenty years without the least success.

The chaplain often confided to us in his sermons that prisoners came to him pretending they had derived great good from his ministrations, only in order to gain some little privilege. I learned, also, from casual conversations in the exercise-ground, that the old gentleman had his favorites, who were not always held in the same esteem and affection by their companions. They were generally regarded as spies and tell-tales, and the men were very cautious of what they said and did in the presence of these elect. Piety was looked upon as a species of humbug, although (so persistent is human nature) a really good, generous man would have been liked and respected. "I could be pious for a pound a day," said one prisoner in my hearing, with reference to the chaplain's salary. "Yes," said the man he spoke to, "so could I, or 'arf of it."

One Sunday the lesson was the story of Peter's miraculous rescue from prison. "Ah," said an old fellow to his pal, "that was a good yarn we heard this morning. I'd like to see th' angel git 'im out o' Holloway."

Parson Plaford was evangelical, but a thorough Churchman, and he had a strong preference for those of his own sect. There was in the prison a young fellow, the son of a wealthy member of Parliament, whose name I need not disclose. He was doing eighteen months for getting into difficulties on the turf, and mistaking his father's name for his own. Having plenty of money, he was able to establish communication with his friends outside; and this being detected, the Governor kept him constantly on the move from wing to wing, and corridor to corridor, so that he might have no time to grow familiar with the officers and corrupt their integrity. The plan was a good one, but it did not succeed. Young officers, who work ninety or a hundred hours a week, with only two off Sundays in three months, for twenty-three shillings, cannot always be expected to resist a bribe.

The young scapegrace I refer to was very anxious to get out of his cell, and he applied to the chaplain for the post of schoolmaster's assistant. The duties of this office are to help bind the books and keep the library catalogue, and to carry the basket of literature when the schoolmaster goes the round. Parson Plaford would not entertain the application. "No," he said, "I begin to think your religious notions are very unsound. I must have a good Churchman for the post." Well, the chaplain got his good Churchman; it was an old hand, sentenced twice before to long terms for felony, and then doing another five or seven years for burglary and assault.

CHAPTER XIV

THE THIRD TRIAL

Prison life is monotonous. Day follows day in weary succession. Except for the card on your door you might lose count of the weeks and forget the date. I went on eating my miserable food with such appetite as I had; I crawled between heaven and earth for one hour in every twenty-four; I picked my fibre to kill the time; and I waded through my only book, the Bible, with the patience of a mule. Weeks rolled by with only one remarkable feature, and that was Good Friday. The "sacred day" was observed as a Sabbath. There was no work and no play. Christians outside were celebrating the Passion of their Redeemer with plenteous eating and copious drinking, and dance and song; while I and my two fellow-prisoners, who had no special cause for sadness on that day, were compelled to spend it like hermits. Chapel hours brought the only relief. Parson Plaford thought it an auspicious occasion for preaching one of his silliest sermons, and when I returned to my cell I was greatly refreshed. Opening my Bible, I read the four accounts of the Crucifixion, and marvelled how so many millions of people could regard them as consistent histories, until I reflected that they never took the trouble to read them one after another at a single sitting.

Once or twice I caught a glimpse of Mr. Ramsey in chapel, and I occasionally saw Mr. Kemp in the exercise-ground. But I knew nothing of what was going on outside. One day, however, the outer silence was broken. The Governor entered my cell in the morning, and told me he had received a letter from Mr. Bradlaugh, stating that our original Indictment (in which he was included) would be tried in a few days, and that he had an order from the Home Office to see Mr. Ramsey and me separately. It was some day early in April; I forget exactly when. But I recollect that Mr. Bradlaugh came up the same afternoon. He saw me in the Governor's office. We shook hands heartily, and plunged into conversation, while the Governor sat turning over papers at his desk.

Mr. Bradlaugh told me how our Indictment stood. It would be tried very soon. He was going to insist on being tried separately, and had no doubt he should be. In that event, his case would precede ours. What did I intend to do? His advice was that I should plead inability to defend myself while in prison, and ask for a postponement until after my release. If that were done he believed I should never hear of the Indictment again.

My view was different. I doubted whether another conviction would add to my sentence, and I was anxious to secure the moral advantage of a careful and spirited defence in the Court of Queen's Bench before the Lord Chief Justice of England. The Governor had already supplied me with writing materials, and I had begun to draw up a list of books I might require, which I intended to send to Mr. Wheeler.

"Oh," said Mr. Bradlaugh, brusquely, "you need not send anything to Mr. Wheeler; he's gone insane."

"What!" I gasped. The room darkened to my vision as though the sun had been blotted out. The blow went to my heart like a dagger.

"Come," said Mr. Bradlaugh in a kinder tone, "if you take the news in that way I shall tell you no more."

"It is over," I answered. "Pray go on."

I crushed down my feelings, but it was not over. Mr. Bradlaugh did not know the nature of my friendship with Mr. Wheeler; how old and deep it was, how inwrought with the roots of my being. When I returned to my cell I went through my agony and bloody sweat. I know not how long it lasted. For awhile I stood like a stone image; anon I paced up and down like a caged tiger. One word burned like a lurid sun through a bloody mist. Mad! The schoolmaster called on business. "Don't speak," I said. He cast a frightened look at my face and retired. At length relief came. The thunder-cloud of grief poured itself in a torrent of tears, the only ones my persecutors ever wrung from me. Over the flood of sorrow rose the rainbow of hope. He is only broken down, I thought; his delicate organisation has succumbed to a trial too great for its strength; rest and generous attention will restore him. Courage! All will be well.

And all is well. My friend is by my side again. He had relapses after his first recovery, for it was an awful blow; but I was in time to shield him from the worst of these. Scientific treatment, and a long stay at the seaside, renovated his frame. He has worked with me daily since at our old task, and I trust we shall labor together till there comes "The poppied sleep, the end of all."

I spent the next few days in preparing a new defence for my third trial for Blasphemy. During that time I was allowed an interview with two friends every afternoon. Mrs. Besant was one of my earliest visitors. I learned that the Freethinker was still appearing under the editorship of Dr. E. B. Aveling, who conducted it until my release; and that the business affairs of Mr. Ramsey and myself were being ably and vigilantly superintended by a committee consisting of Mrs. Besant, and Messrs. R. O. Smith, A. Hilditch, J. Grout, G. Standring and C. Herbert. There was, in addition, a Prisoners' Aid Fund opened and liberally subscribed to, out of which our wives and families were provided for.

On the morning of April 10, soon after breakfast, and while the prisoners were marshalling for chapel, I was conducted to a cell in front of the gaol, and permitted to array myself once more in a civilized costume. My clothes, like myself, were none the better for their imprisonment; but I felt a new man as I donned them, and trolled operatic airs, while warder Smith cried, "Hush!"

Mr. Ramsey went through a similar process. We met in the great hall, and in defiance of all rules and regulations, I shook him heartily by the hand. He looked thin, pale, and careworn; and the new growth of hair on his chin did not add to his good looks. After our third trial he got stout again, and it was I who scaled less and less. Perhaps his shoemaking gave him a better appetite; and perhaps I studied too much for the quantity and quality of prison blood.

Each of was accommodated with a four-wheeler, and a warder armed with a cutlass to guard us from all danger. It was a beautiful spring morning, and the sunlight looked glorious as we rattled down the Caledonian Road. I felt new-born. The early flowers in the street barrows were miracles of loveliness, and the very vegetables had a supernal charm. Tradesmen's names over their shops were wonderfully vivid. Every letter seemed fresh-painted, and after the dinginess of prison, the crude decorations struck me as worthy of the old masters.

Arriving at the rear of the Law Courts, we found many friends awaiting us. Colonel Milman was obliged to protect us from their demonstrations of welcome. Everyone of them seemed desirous to wring off an arm as a souvenir of the occasion. Inside I met Mr. Bradlaugh, Mrs. Besant, Dr. Aveling, and a host of other friends. My wife looked pale and haggard. She had evidently suffered much. But seeing me again was a great relief, and she bore the remainder of her long trial with more cheerfulness.

Mr. Bradlaugh's trial lasted three days, and we were brought up on each occasion. It was what the Americans call a fine time. A grateful country found us in cabs and attendants, and our friends found us in dinner. When the first day's adjournment came at one o'clock, my counsel, Mr. Cluer, asked what he should order for us. "What a question!" we cried. "Something soon, and plenty of it." It was boiled mutton, turnips, and potatoes. We proved ourselves excellent trenchermen, for it was our first square meal for weeks; and a group, including some of the jury, watched us feed.

Lord Coleridge's summing up in Mr. Bradlaugh's case was a wonderful piece of art. The even beauty of his voice, the dignity of his manner, the pathetic gravity with which he appealed to the jury to cast aside all prejudice against the defendant, combined to render his charge one of the great memories of my life.

The jury retired for half an hour, and returned with a verdict of Not Guilty! Mr. Bradlaugh was deeply affected. I shook his hand without a word, for I was speechless. I was inexpressibly glad that the enemy had not crippled him in his parliamentary struggle, and that his recent victory in the House of Lords, after years of litigation, was crowned by a happy escape from their worst design.

Our trial took place the next week, and lasted only two days, as we had no technical points to argue. Mr. Wheeler came up from Worcestershire to see me. He was still very weak, and obviously suffering from intense excitement. Still it was a pleasure to see his face and clasp his hand.

Sir Hardinge Giffard gloomed on us with his wintry face, but he left the conduct of the case almost entirely to Mr. Maloney. The evidence against us was overpowering, and we did not seriously contest it. Mr. Ramsey read a brief speech after lunch, and precisely at two o'clock I rose to make my defence, which lasted two hours and forty minutes.

The table before me was crowded with books and papers, and I held a sheet of references that looked like a brief. My first step was to pay Judge North an instalment of the debt I owed him.

> *"My lord, and gentlemen of the jury,—I am very happy, not to stand in this position, but to learn what I had not learned before—how a criminal trial should be conducted, notwithstanding that two months ago I was tried in another court, and before another judge. Fortunately, the learned counsel, who are conducting this prosecution have not now a judge who will allow them to walk out of court while he argues their brief for them in their absence."*

Lord Coleridge interrupted me. "You must learn one more lesson, Mr. Foote, and that is, that one judge cannot hear another judge censured, or even commended."

I was checkmated, but taking it with a good grace, I said:

> *"My lord, thank you for the correction. And I will simply confine the observations I might have made on that subject to*

the emphatic statement that I have learnt to-day, for the first time—although this is the second time I have had to answer a criminal charge—how a criminal trial should be conducted."

His lordship did not interrupt me again. During the whole of my long defence he leaned his head upon his hand, and looked steadily at me, without once shifting his gaze.

To put the jury in a good frame of mind I told them that two months before I fell among thieves, and congratulated myself on being able to talk to twelve honest men. In order, also, that they might be disabused of the idea that we were being treated as first-class misdemeanants, I informed them of the discipline we were really subjected to; and I saw that this aroused their sympathy.

Those who wish to read my defence in extenso will find it in the "Three Trials for Blasphemy." I shall content myself here with a few points. I quoted heretical, and, as I contended, blasphemous passages from the writings of Professor Huxley, Dr. Maudsley, Herbert Spencer, John Stuart Mill, Matthew Arnold, Lord Amberly, the Duke of Somerset, Shelley, Byron, James Thomson, Algernon Swinburne, and others; and I urged that the only difference between these passages and the incriminated parts of my paper consisted in the price t which they were published. Why, I asked, should the high-class blasphemer be petted by society, and the low-class blasphemer be made to bear their sins, and driven forth into the wilderness of Holloway Gaol?

Lord Coleridge, in his summing up, supported my view, and his admission is so important that I venture to give it in full.

> *"With regard to some of the others from whom Mr. Foote quoted passages, I heard many of them for the first time. I do not at all question that Mr. Foote read them correctly. They are passages which, hearing them only from him for the first time, I confess I have a difficulty in distinguishing from the incriminated publication. They do appear to me to be open to exactly the same charge and the same grounds of observation that Mr. Foote's publications are. He says—and I don't call upon him to prove it, I am quite willing to take his word—he says many of these things are written in expensive books, published by publishers of known eminence, and that they circulate in the drawing-rooms, studies, and libraries of persons of position. It may be so. All I can say here is— and so far I can answer for myself—I would make no distinction between Mr. Foote and anybody else; and if there are persons, however eminent they may be, who used language, not fairly distinguishable from that used by Mr. Foote, and if they are*

ever brought before me—which I hope they never may be, for a more troublesome or disagreeable business can never be inflicted upon me—if they come before me, so far as my poor powers go they shall have neither more nor less than the justice I am trying to do to Mr. Foote; and if they offend the Blasphemy Laws they shall find that so long as these laws exist—whatever I may think about their wisdom—they will have but one rule of law laid down in this court."

Another point I raised, which I neglected in my previous defences, was this. What is it that men have a right to at law?

"Every man has a right to three things—protection for person, property and character, and all that can be legitimately derived from these. The ordinary law of libel gives a man protection for his character, but it is surely monstrous that he should claim protection for his opinions and tastes. All that he can claim is that his taste shall not be violently outraged against his will. I hope, gentlemen, you will take that rational view of the question. We have libelled no man's character, we have invaded no man's person or property. This crime is a constructed crime, originally manufactured by priests in the interest of their own order to put down dissent and heresy. It now lingers amongst us as a legacy utterly alien to the spirit of our age, which unfortunately we have not resolution enough to cast among those absurdities which Time holds in his wallet of oblivion."

My peroration is the only other part of the defence which I shall extract.

"Gentlemen, I have more than a personal interest in the result of this trial. I am anxious for the rights and liberties of thousands of my countrymen. Young as I am, I have for many years fought for my principles, taken soldier's wages when there were any, and gone cheerfully without when there were none, and fought on all the same, as I mean to do to the end; and I am doomed to the torture of twelve months' imprisonment by the verdict and judgment of thirteen men, whose sacrifices for conviction may not equal mine. The bitterness of my fate can scarcely be enhanced by your verdict. Yet this does not diminish my solicitude as to its character. If, after the recent scandalous proceedings in another court, you, as a special jury in this High Court of Justice, bring in a verdict of Guilty against me and my co-defendant, you will decisively inaugurate a new era of persecution, in which no advantage can accrue to truth or morality, but in which fierce passions will be kindled,

> oppression and resistance matched against each other, and the land perhaps disgraced with violence and stained with blood. But if, as I hope, you return a verdict of Not Guilty, you will check that spirit of bigotry and fanaticism which is fully aroused and eagerly awaiting the signal to begin its evil work; you will close a melancholy and discreditable chapter of history; you will proclaim that henceforth the press shall be absolutely free, unless it libel men's characters or contain incitements to crime, and that all offences against belief and taste shall be left to the great jury of public opinion; you will earn the gratitude of all who value liberty as the jewel of their souls, and independence as the crown of their manhood; you will save your country from becoming ridiculous in the eyes of nations that we are accustomed to consider as less enlightened and free; and you will earn for yourselves a proud place in the annals of its freedom, its progress, and its glory."

I delivered this appeal to the jury as impressively as I could. There was a solemn silence in court. A storm cloud gathered while I spoke, and heavy drops of rain fell on the roof as I concluded.

Lord Coleridge lifted his elbow from his desk, and addressed the jury:

> "Gentlemen, I should have been glad to have summed up this evening, but the truth is, I am not very strong, and I propose to address you in the morning, and that will give you a full opportunity of reflecting calmly on the very striking and able speech you have just heard."

My defence was a great effort, and it exhausted me. Until I had to exert myself I did not know how the confinement and the prison fare had weakened me. The reader will understand the position better if I remind him that the only material preparation I had in the morning for the task of defending myself against Sir Hardinge Giffard and Mr. Maloney was six ounces of dry bread and a little thin cocoa, which the doctor had ordered instead of the "skilly" to stop my diarrhoea. The Governor kindly allowed one of my friends to fetch me a little brandy. Then we drove back to prison, where I had some more dry bread and thin cocoa. The next morning, after an exactly similar meal, we drove down again to the court.

Lord Coleridge's summing-up lasted nearly two hours, and, like my defence, it was listened to by a crowded court, which included a large number of gentlemen of the wig and gown. His lordship's address is reported at length in the "Three Trials for Blasphemy," and a revised copy was published by himself. His view of the law has been dealt with already in my Preface. What I wish to say here is, that Lord Coleridge's demeanor was in marked contrast with Judge North's. I cannot do better than quote a few passages from an open letter I addressed to his lordship soon after my release:

> "How were my feelings modified by your lordship's lofty bearing! I found myself in the presence of a judge who was a gentleman. You treated me with impartiality, and a generous consideration for my misfortunes. No one could doubt your sincerity when, in the midst of a legal illustration which might be construed as a reflection on my character, you suddenly checked yourself, and said, 'I mean no offence to Mr. Foote. I should be unworthy of my position if I insulted anyone in his.' You were scrupulously, almost painfully, careful to say nothing that could assist the prosecution or wound my susceptibilities. You appeared to tremble lest your own convictions should prejudice you, and the jury through you, against me and my fellow prisoner. You listened with the deepest attention to my long address to the jury. You discussed all my arguments that you considered essential in your summing-up; and you strengthened some of them, while deprecating others, with a logical force and beauty of expression which were at once my admiration and my despair. You paid me such handsome compliments on my defence in the most trying circumstances as dispelled at once the orthodox theory that I was a mere vulgar criminal. In brief, my lord, you displayed such a lofty spirit of justice, such a tenderness of humanity, and such a dignity of bearing, that you commanded my admiration, my reverence and my love; and if the jury had convicted me, and your lordship had felt obliged by the 'unpleasant law' to inflict upon me some measure of punishment, I could still have kissed the hand that dealt the blow.
>
> "I know how repulsive flattery must be to a nature like yours, but your lordship will pardon one who is no sycophant, who seeks neither to avert your frown nor to gain your favor, who has no sinister object in view, but simply speaks from the fulness of a grateful heart. And you will pardon me if I say that my sentiments are shared by thousands, who hate your creed but respect your character. They watched you throughout my trial with the keenest interest, and they rejoiced when they saw in you those noble human qualities which transcend all dogmas and creeds, and dwarf all differences of opinion into absolute insignificance."

Lord Coleridge also deserves my thanks for the handsome manner in which he seconded my efforts to repudiate the odious charge of "indecency," which had been manufactured by the bigots after my imprisonment. These are his lordship's words:

> "Mr. Foote is anxious to have it impressed on your minds that he is not a licentious writer, and that this word does not fairly apply to his publications. You will have the documents before you, and you must judge for yourselves. I should say that he is right. He may be blasphemous, but he certainly is not licentious, in the ordinary sense of the word; and you do not find him pandering to the bad passions of mankind."

I ask my readers to notice these clear and emphatic sentences, for we shall recur to them in the next chapter.

The jury retired at twenty minutes past twelve. At three minutes past five they were discharged, being unable to agree. It was a glorious victory. Acquittal was hopeless, but no verdict amounted practically to the same thing. Two juries out of three had already disagreed, and as the verdict of Guilty by the third had been won through the scandalous partiality and mean artifices of a bigoted judge, the results of our prosecution afforded little encouragement to fresh attacks on the liberty of the press.

I have since had the pleasure of conversing with one of the jury. Himself and two others held out against a verdict of Guilty, and he told me that the discussion was extremely animated. My informant acted on principle. He confessed he did not like my caricatures, and he considered my attacks on the Bible too severe; but he held that I had a perfect right to ridicule Christianity if I thought fit, and he refused to treat any method of attacking opinions as a crime. Of the other two jurors, one was convinced by my address, and the other declared that he was not going to assist in imprisoning like a thief "a man who could make a speech like that."

The next day I asked Lord Coleridge not to try the case again for a few days, as I was physically unable to conduct my defence. His lordship said:

> "I have just been informed, and I hardly knew it before, what such imprisonment as yours means, and what, in the form it has been inflicted on you, it must mean; but now that I do know of it, I will take care that the proper authorities know of it also, and I will see that you have proper support."

His lordship added that he would see I had proper food, and

he would take the defence whenever I pleased. We fixed the following Tuesday. During the interim our meals were provided from the public-house opposite the prison gates. My diarrhoea ceased at once, and I so far recovered my old form that I felt ready to fight twenty Giffards. But we did not encounter each other again. Feeling assured that if Lord Coleridge continued to try the case, as he obviously meant to until it was disposed of, they would never obtain a verdict, the prosecution secured a nolle prosequi from the Attorney-General. It was procured by means of an affidavit, containing what his lordship branded as an absolute falsehood. So the prosecution, which began in bigotry and malice, ended appropriately in a lie.

CHAPTER XV

LOSS AND GAIN

Our victory in the Court of Queen's Bench was an unmitigated loss to Sir Henry Tyler and his backers, for it threw upon them the whole costs of the prosecution. It was also a loss to ourselves; for I have it on the best authority that, if we had been found guilty, Lord Coleridge would have made his sentence concurrent with Judge North's, and shifted us from the criminal to the civil side of the prison, where we should have enjoyed each other's society, worn our own clothes, eaten our own food, seen our friends frequently, received and answered letters, and spent our time in rational occupations. To the Freethought cause, however, our victory was a pure gain. As I had anticipated, the press gave our new trial a good deal of attention. The Daily News printed a leading article on the case, calling on the Home Secretary to remit the rest of our sentence. The Times published a long and admirable report of my defence, as well as of Lord Coleridge's summing-up, and predicted that the trial would be historical, "chiefly because of the remarkable defence made by one of the defendants." A similar prediction appeared in the Manchester Weekly Times, according to which "the defendant Foote argued his case with consummate skill." Across the Atlantic, the New York World said that "Mr. Foote, in particular, delivered a speech which, for closeness of argument and vividness of presentation, has not often been equalled." Even the grave and reverend Westminster Review found "after reading what the Lord Chief Justice himself characterises as Mr. Foote's very striking and able speech, that the editor of the Freethinker is very far from being the vulgar and uneducated disputant which the Spectator appears to have supposed him." Other Liberal papers, like the Pall Mall Gazette and the Referee, that had at first joined in the chorus of execration over the fallen "blasphemer," now found that my sentence was "monstrous."

So true is it that nothing succeeds like success! I did not let these compliments turn my head. My speeches at the Old Bailey were little, if anything, inferior to the one I made in the Court of Queen's Bench. There was no change in me, but only in the platform I spoke from. The great fact to my mind was this, that given an impartial judge, and a fair trial, it was difficult to convict any

Freethinker of "blasphemy" if he could only defend himself with some courage and address. This fact shone like a star of hope in the night of my suffering. As I said in one of my three letters from prison: "For the first time juries have disagreed, and chances are already slightly against a verdict of Guilty. Now the jury is the hand by which the enemy grasps us, and when we have absolutely secured the twelfth man we shall have amputated the thumb."

On May 1 the following letter from Admiral Maxse appeared in the Daily News:

"TO THE EDITOR OF THE 'DAILY NEWS.'

SIR,—Foote's brilliant defence last week will probably have awakened some fastidious critics to their error in having depicted him as a low and coarse controversialist, while Lord Coleridge's judgment will have convinced the public that had Lord Coleridge occupied the place of Justice North, the defendant would have escaped with a mild penalty. In the meantime, Mr. Foote continues to undergo what is virtually 'solitary confinement' in a cell, and is condemned to this punishment for a year. A more wicked sentence, or a more wicked law, than the one which Mr. Foote and his companions suffer from, is, in my opinion, impossible to conceive, that is to say in a country which professes to enjoy religious liberty. His crime consisted in caricaturing a grotesque representation of a religion which has certainly a higher side. People who are truly religious should be obliged to Mr. Foote, if he managed to shock some people concerning any feature of religion which is gross and degrading to that religion. I know something of Mr. Foote, and I am quite certain he would not say anything to shock a refined interpretation of religion. Refined Christians are anxious themselves to get rid of the excrescences of their creed. The question at issue really is as to whether a coarse picture of religion, and of one religion only, is to be protected by the State from caricature, and from caricature alone; because it seems to be granted that an intellectual absurdity may be intellectually impeached. It is impossible such a monstrous doctrine as this can stand. It will pass away, and probably in a few years it will be remembered with some astonishment; but oppressive and persecuting laws are only got rid of by the spectacle of an impaled victim. 'By the light of burning heretics Christ's bleeding feet I track.' The impaled victim is now Mr. Foote. It is a disgrace to England that his solitary confinement—twenty-three out of the twenty-four hours are solitary—or indeed, that any punishment whatever is possible for a man's style in religious controversy; and to a Liberal it is profoundly humiliating that such a proceeding

takes place under a Liberal Government and without one word of remonstrance in the House of Commons. Where are the Radicals?— Yours obediently,
FREDK. A. MAXSE
"April 30th"

Let me take this opportunity of thanking Admiral Maxse for his courageous generosity on my behalf. Directly he heard of my infamous sentence he wrote me a brave letter, which the prison rules forbade my receiving, stating that he would join in any agitation for my release, or for the repeal of the wretched law under which I was suffering "the utmost martyrdom which society can at present impose." I have always regarded Admiral Maxse as one of the purest and noblest of our public men, and I valued his sympathy even more than his assistance.

Further correspondence appeared in the Daily News, and the Liberal papers called on Sir William Harcourt to intervene. Memorials for our release flowed in from all parts of the country. One of these deserves especial mention. The signatures were procured, at great expense of time and labor, by Dr. E. B. Aveling and an eminent psychologist who desired to avoid publicity. Among them I find the following names:—

Admiral Maxse George Bullen C. Crompton, Q.C. George Du Maurier Charles Maclaren, M.P. George Dixon Dr. G. J. Romanes Henry Sidgwick. Dr. Charlton Bastian Herbert Spencer Dr. Edward Clodd Hon. E. Lyulph Stanley, M.P. Dr. E. B. Tylor J. Cotter Morison Dr. W. Aldis Wright Jonathan Hutchinson Dr. Macallister John Collier Dr. E. Bond John Pettie Dr. J. H. Jackson James Sully Dr. H. Maudsley Leslie Stephen Editor Daily News Lient.-Col. Osborne Editor Spectator P. A. Taylor, M.P. Editor Academy Professor Alexander Bain Editor Manchester Examiner Professor Huxley Editor Liverpool Daily Post Professor Tyndall Francis Galton Professor Knight F. Guthrie, F.R.S. Professor E. S. Beesly Frederick Harrison Professor H. S. Foxwell G. H. Darwin Professor R. Adamson Professor G. Croom Robertson Rev. Dr. Fairbairn Professor E. Ray Lancaster Rev. R. Glover Professor Drummond Rev. J. G. Rogers Professor T. Rhys Davids Rev. J. Aldis R. H. Moncrieff Rev. Charles Beard Rev. J. Llewellyn Davies Rev. Dr. Crosskey Rev. Dr. Abbot S. H. Vines Rev. A. Ainger The Mayor of Birmingham Rev. Stopford A. Brooke

I doubt whether such a memorial, signed by so many illustrious men, was ever before presented to a Home Secretary for the release of any prisoners. But it made no impression on Sir William Harcourt, for the simple reason that the signatories were not politicians, but only men of genius. As the Weekly Dispatch said, "Sir William Harcourt never does the right thing when he has a chance of going wrong." The Echo also "regretted" the Home Secretary's decision, while the Pall Mall Gazette, then under the editorship of Mr. John Morley, concluded its article on the subject by saying, "The fact remains that Mr. Foote is suffering a scandalously excessive punishment, and that the Home Office must now share the general condemnation that has hitherto been confined to the judge."

On July 11 a mass meeting was held in St. James's Hall to protest against our continued imprisonment. Despite the summer weather, the huge building was crammed with people, every inch of standing room being occupied, and thousands turned away from the doors. Letters of sympathy were sent by Canon Shuttleworth, Admiral Maxse and Mr. P. A. Taylor M.P. Among the speakers were the Rev. W. Sharman, the Rev. S. D. Headlam, the Rev. E. M. Geldart, Mr. C. Bradlaugh M.P., Mrs. Annie Besant, Dr. E. B. Aveling, Mr. Joseph Symes, Mr. Moncure D. Conway and Mr. H. Burrows. The greatest enthusiasm prevailed, and the resolutions were carried with only two dissentients.

Still Sir William Harcourt made no sign. At last Mr. Peter Taylor, the honored member for Leicester, publicly interrogated the Home Secretary in the House of Commons. Mr. Taylor's question was as follows:

"Mr. P. A. TAYLOR asked the Secretary of State for the Home Department whether he had received memorials from many thousands of persons, including clergymen of the Church of England, Nonconformist ministers, and persons of high literary and scientific position, asking for a mitigation of the sentences of George William Foote and William James Ramsey, now imprisoned in Holloway Gaol on a charge of blasphemy; whether they have already suffered five months' imprisonment, involving until lately confinement in their respective cells for twenty-three hours out of every twenty-four, and now involving twenty-two hours of such solitary confinement out of each 24; and whether he will advise the remission of the remainder of their sentences."

Thereupon Sir William Harcourt reared his unblushing front and gave this answer:

"Sir WILLIAM HARCOURT—The question of my hon. friend is founded upon misconception of the duties and rights of the Secretary of State in reference to sentences of the law, which I have often endeavoured to remove, but apparently with entire want of success.

It is perfectly true that I have received many memorials on this subject, most of them founded on misconception of the law on which the sentence rested. This is not a matter I can take into consideration, either upon my own opinion or upon that of 'clergymen of the Church of England, Nonconformist ministers, and persons of high literary and scientific position.' I am bound to assume that until Parliament alters the law that law is right, and that those who administer the law administer it rightly. If I took any other course, outside my opinion—if I had one upon this subject—I should be interfering with the making and with the administration of the law, and transferring it from Parliament to the Executive and to a Minister of the Crown. I am quite sure my hon. friend would not like that course. It has been said, "Oh, but you can deal with sentences." (Hear, hear.) Sentences must be dealt with not upon the assumption that the law was wrong, and that the jury and judge were wrong, but upon special circumstances applicable to the particular case which would justify a Minister in recommending to the Crown a remission of sentence. What are the circumstances? Nobody—I do not care whether legal persons or belonging to the classes mentioned in this question—who has not seen the publication can judge of the matter. I have seen it, and I have no hesitation in saying that it is in the most strict sense of the word an obscene libel. It is a scandalous outrage upon public decency. (Opposition cheers.) That being so, the law has declared that it is punishable by law. I have no authority to declare that the law shall not be obeyed; nor do I think that within less than half the period of the punishment awarded by the Court, if I were to advise the Crown to remit the sentence, I should be discharging the responsibility which rests upon me with a sound or sober judgment. (Opposition cheers, and murmurs below the gangway.)"

The Tory cheers which greeted this malicious reply suffice to condemn it. Sir William Harcourt has told many lies in his time, but this was the most brazen of all. He knew we were not prosecuted for obscenity; he knew there was not a suggestion of indecency in our indictment; and he had before him the distinct language of the Lord Chief Justice of England, exonerating us from the slander. Yet he deliberately libelled us, in a place where his utterances are privileged, in order to conciliate the Tories and please the bigots. Some of the Radical papers protested against this wanton misrepresentation, but I am not aware that a single Christian journal censured the lie which was used to justify persecution.

Freethinkers have not forgotten Sir William Harcourt, nor have I. Some day we may be able to punish him for the insult. Meanwhile, I venture to think that if the member for Derby and the editor of the Freethinker were placed side by side, an unprejudiced stranger would have little difficulty in deciding which of the two was the more likely to be bestial.

Poor Mr. Ramsey, not knowing his man, innocently petitioned the Home Secretary from prison, pointing out that he was tried and imprisoned for blasphemy, asking to be released at once, and offering to supply Sir William Harcourt with fresh copies of our Christmas Number for a new trial for obscenity. Of course he received no reply.

My counsel, Mr. Cluer, gallantly defended my reputation in the columns of the Daily News, and he was supported by one of the Jury, who wrote as follows:

> *"SIR,—From the reference in your short leader on the subject, it appears that the Home Secretary, in answer to Mr. Taylor, declined to consent to the release of Messrs. Foote and Ramsey, on the ground that they had published an obscene libel. On the late trial before the Lord Chief Justice, certain numbers of the Freethinker, on which the prisoners were being tried, were charged by the prosecution with being (inter alia) blasphemous and indecent. The judge in the course of his remarks said, the articles inculpated might be blasphemous, but assuredly they were not indecent. The opinion of Sir William Harcourt, consequently, though in harmony with that of the junior counsel for the prosecution, is altogether opposed to that of Lord Coleridge, who was the judge in the case."*

The Daily News itself put the matter very clearly. "Mr. Foote and Mr. Ramsey," it said, "were sent to prison by Mr. Justice North for publishing a blasphemous libel. Sir William Harcourt declines to release them on the ground that they have published an obscene libel. It is not usual to keep Englishmen in gaol on the ground that they committed an offence of which they have not been convicted, and against which they have had no opportunity of defending themselves." But Sir William Harcourt thought otherwise, and kept us in prison, acting at once as prosecutor, witness, jury and judge.

Mr. Gladstone was appealed to, but he "regretted he could do nothing," presumably because we were only Englishmen and not Bulgarians. An answer to this piece of callous hypocrisy came from the London clubs. One resolution passed by the Combined Radical Clubs of Chelsea, representing thousands of working men, characterised our continued imprisonment as an indelible stigma on the Liberal Government.

CHAPTER XVI

A LONG NIGHT

Feeling there was no prospect of release, and resigned to my fate, I settled down to endure it, with a resolution to avail myself of every possible mitigation. Colonel Milman included us among the special exercise men, and we enjoyed the luxury of two outings every day; our solitary confinement being thus reduced to twenty-two hours instead of twenty-three. By finessing I also managed to get an old feather pillow from the store-room, which proved a comfortable addition to the wooden bolster. The alteration in our food I have already mentioned.

Sir William Harcourt did absolutely nothing for us, but the Secretary of the Prison Commissioners gave instructions that we were to be treated as kindly as possible, so that "nothing might happen" to us. One of the upper officers, whom I have seen since, told me we were a source of great anxiety to the authorities, and they were very glad to see our backs.

Mr. Anderson called on me in my cell and asked what he could do for me.

"Open the front door," I answered.

With a pleasant smile he regretted his inability to do that.

"Well then," I continued, "let me have something to read."

"Yes," he said, "I can do that. There are many books in the prison library."

"But not one," I retorted, "fit for an educated man to read. They are all selected by the chaplain."

"Well," he answered, "I cannot give you what we haven't got."

"But why not let me have my own books to read?" I asked.

Mr. Anderson replied that such a thing was unheard of, but I persisted in my plea, which Colonel Milman generously supported.

"Well," said Mr. Anderson, "I suppose we must. Your own books may be sent in, and the Governor can let you have them two at a time. But, you know, you mustn't have such writings as you are here for."

"Oh," I replied, "you have the power to check that. They will all pass through the Governor's hands, and I will order in nothing but what Colonel Milman might read himself."

"Oh," said Mr. Anderson, with a humorous smile, which the Governor and the Inspector shared, "I can't say what Colonel Milman might like to read."

The interview ended and my books came. What a joy they were! I read Gibbon and Mosheim right through again, with Carlyle's "Frederick," "French Revolution" and "Cromwell," Forster's "Statesmen of the Commonwealth," and a mass of literature on the Rebellion and the Protectorate. I dug deep into the literature of Evolution. I read over again all Shakespeare, Shelley, Spenser, Swift and Byron, besides a number of more modern writers. French books were not debarred, so I read Diderot, Voltaire, Paul Louis Courier, and the whole of Flaubert, including "L'Education Sentimentale," which I never attacked before, but which I found, after conquering the apparent dullness of the first half of the first volume, to be one of the greatest of his triumphs. Mr. Gerald Massey, then on a visit to England, was churlishly refused a visiting order from the Home Office, but he sent me his two magnificent volumes on "Natural Genesis," and a note to the interim editor of the Freethinker, requesting him to tell me that I had his sympathy. "I fight the same battle as himself," said Mr. Massey, "although with a somewhat different weapon." I was also favored with a presentation copy of verses by the one writer I most admire, whose genius I reverenced long before the public and its critics discovered it. It would gratify my vanity rather than my prudence to reveal his name.

Agreeably to the proverb that if you give some men an inch they will take an ell, I induced the Governor to let me pursue my study of Italian. First he allowed me a Grammar, then a Conversation Book, then a Dictionary, then a Prose Reading Book, and then a Poetical Anthology. These volumes, being an addition to the two ordinary ones, gave my little domicile a civilised appearance. Cleaners sometimes, when my door was opened, looked in from the corridor with an expression of awe. "Why," I heard one say, "he's got a cell like a bookshop."

With my books, my Italian, and my Colenso, I managed to kill the time; and although the snake-like days were still long, they were less venomous. Yet the remainder of my sentence was a terrible ordeal. I never lost heart, but I lost strength. My brain was miraculously clear, but it grew weaker as the body languished; and before my release I could hardly read more than an hour or two a day.

The only break in the monotony of my life was when I received a visit. Mrs. Besant, Dr. Aveling, Mr. Wheeler and my wife, saw me occasionally; either in the ordinary way, at the end of every three months, or by special order from the Home Office. I saw my visitors in the prison cages, only our faces being visible to each other through a narrow slit. We stood about six feet apart, with a warder between us to stop "improper conversation." I could not shake a friend's hand or kiss my wife. The interviews lasted only half an hour. In the middle of a sentence "Time!" was shouted, the keys rattled, and the little oasis had to be left for another journey over the desert sand.

Every three months I wrote a letter on a prison sheet. Two sides were printed on, and the others ruled wide, with a notice that nothing was to be written between the lines. No doubt the authorities were anxious to save the prisoners the pain of too much mental exertion. I foiled them by writing small, and abbreviating nearly every word. My letters were of course read before they were sent out, and the answers read before they reached me. No respect being shown for the privacies of affection, I addressed my letters to Dr. Aveling for publication in the Freethinker.

One of these documents lies before me as I write. It was the extra letter I sent to my wife before leaving, and contains directions as to clothes and other domestic matters. I venture to reproduce the advertisement, which occupies the whole front page:

"A prisoner is permitted to write and receive a Letter after three months of his sentence have expired, provided his conduct and industry have been satisfactory during that time, and the same privilege will be continued afterwards on the same conditions and at the same intervals.

"All Letters of an improper or idle tendency, either to or from Prisoners, or containing slang or other objectionable expressions, will be suppressed. The permission to write and receive letters is given to the Prisoners for the purpose of enabling them to keep up a connexion with their respectable friends, and not that they may hear the news of the day.

"All Letters are read by the Authorities of the Prison, and must be legibly written, and not crossed.

"Neither clothes, money, nor any other articles, are allowed to be received by any Officers of the Prison for the use of Prisoners; all parcels containing such articles intended for Prisoners on discharge must bear outside the name of the Prisoner, and be sent to the Governor, or they will not be received. Persons attempting otherwise to introduce any article to or for a prisoner, are liable to a fine or imprisonment, and the Prisoner concerned may be severely punished."

The authorities are not so careful about the letter being legible by its recipient. They do not insert it in an envelope, but just fold it up and fasten it with a little gum, so that the letter is nearly sure to be torn in the opening. The address is written on the back by the prisoner himself, before the sheet is folded. Lines are provided for the purpose, and it is pretty easy to see what the letter is. Surely a little more consideration might be shown for a prisoner's friends. They are not criminals, and as the prison authorities incur the expense of postage, they might throw in a cheap envelope without ruining the nation.

Mr. Kemp was released on May 25 in a state of exhaustion. It is doubtful if he could have survived another three months' torture. What illness in the frightful solitude of a prison cell is I know. I once caught a bad cold, and for the first time in my life had the toothache. It came on about two o'clock in the afternoon, and as applications for the doctor are only received before breakfast, I had to wait until the next day before I could obtain relief. It arrived of itself about one o'clock. The doctor had considerately left my case till last, in order to give me proper attention.

Mr. Ramsey was released on November 24. He was welcomed at the prison gates by a crowd of sympathisers, and entertained at a breakfast in the Hall of Science, where he made an interesting speech. By a whimsical calculation, I reckoned that I had still to swallow twenty-one gallons of prison tea and twelve prison sermons.

Christmas Day was the only variation in the remainder of my "term." Being regarded as a Sabbath, it was a day of idleness. The fibre was removed from my cell, my apartment was clean and tidy, a bit of dubbin gave an air of newness to my old shoes, and after a good wash and an energetic use of my three-inch comb, I was ready for the festivities of the season. After a sumptuous breakfast on dry bread, and sweet water misnamed tea, I took a walk in the yard; and on returning to my cell I sat down and wondered how my poor wife was spending the auspicious day. What a "merry Christmas" for a woman whose husband was eating his heart out in gaol! The chapel-bell roused me from phantasy. While the other half of the prison was engaged in "devotion," I did an hour's grinding at Italian, and read a chapter of Gibbon; after which I heard the "miserable sinners" return from the chapel to their cells.

My Christmas dinner consisted of the usual diet, and after eating it I went for another brief tramp in the yard. The officers seemed to relax their usual rigor, and many of the prisoners exchanged greetings. "How did yer like the figgy duff?" "Did the beef stick in yer ribs?" Such were the flowers of conversation. From the talk I overheard, I gathered that under the old management, while Holloway Gaol was the City Prison, all the inmates had a "blow-out" on Christmas Day, in the shape of beef, vegetables, plum-pudding, and a pint of beer. Some of the old hands, who remembered those happy days, bitterly bewailed the decay of prison hospitality. Their lamentations were worthy of a Conservative orator at a rural meeting. The present was a poor thing compared with the past, and they sighed for "the tender grace of a day that is dead."

After exercise I went to chapel. Parson Plaford preached a seasonable sermon, which would have been more heartily relished on a full stomach. He told us what a blessed time Christmas was, and that people did well to be joyful on the anniversary of their Savior's birth. Before dismissing us with his blessing to our "little rooms," which was his habitual euphemism for our cells, he remarked that he could not wish us a happy Christmas in our unhappy condition, but he would wish us a peaceful Christmas; and he ventured to promise us that boon if, after leaving chapel, we fell on our knees and besought pardon for our sins. Most of the prisoners received this advice with a grin, for their cell floors were black-leaded, and genuflexions in their "little rooms" gave them too much knee-cap to their trousers.

At six o'clock I had my third instalment of Christmas fare, the last mouthfuls being consumed to the accompaniment of church bells. The neighboring Bethels were announcing their evening performance, and the sound penetrated into my cell. True believers were wending their way to church, while the heretic, who had dared to deride their creed and denounce their hypocrisy, was regaling himself on dry bread in one of their dungeons. The bells rang out against each other with a wild glee as I paced my narrow floor. They seemed mad with intoxication of victory; they mocked me with a bacchanalian frenzy of triumph. Yet I smiled grimly, for their clamor was no more than the ancient fool's shout, "Great is Diana of the Ephesians." Great Christ has had his day since, but he in turn is dead; dead in man's intellect, dead in man's heart, dead in man's life; a mere phantom, flitting about the aisles of churches, where priestly mummers go through the rites of a phantom creed.

I took my prison Bible and read the story of Christ's birth in Matthew and Luke, Mark and John having never heard of it or forgotten it. What an incongruous jumble of absurdities! A poor fairy tale of the world's childhood, utterly insignificant beside the stupendous revelations of science. From the fanciful story of the Magi following a star to Shelley's "World on worlds are rolling ever," what an advance! As I retired to sleep on my plank-bed my mind was full of these reflections, and when the gas was turned out, and I was left in darkness and silence, I felt serene and almost happy.

CHAPTER XVII

DAYLIGHT

A new day dawned for me on the twenty-fifth of February. I rose as usual a few minutes before six. It was the morning of my release, or in prison language my "discharge." Yet I felt no excitement. I was as calm as my cell walls. "Strange!" the reader will say. Yet not so strange after all. Every day had been filled with expectancy, and anticipation had discounted the reality.

Instead of waiting till eight o'clock, the usual breakfast hour, superintendent Burchell brought my last prison meal at seven. I wondered at his haste, but when he came again, a few minutes later, to see if I had done, I saw through the game. The authorities wished to "discharge" me rapidly, before the hour when my friends would assemble at the prison gates, and so lessen the force of the demonstration. I slackened speed at once, drank my tea in sips, and munched my dry bread with great deliberation. "Come," said superintendent Burchell, "you're very slow this morning." "Oh," I replied, "there's no hurry; after twelve months of it a few minutes make little difference." Burchell put the words and my smile together, and gave the game up.

Down in the bathroom at the foot of the debtors' wing my clothes were set out, and some kind hand had spread a piece of bright carpet for my feet. I dressed very leisurely. With equal tardiness I went through the ceremony of receiving my effects, carefully checking every article, and counting the money coin by coin. The Governor tendered me half a sovereign, the highest sum a prisoner can earn. "Thank you," I said, "but I can't take their money." We had to go through the farce.

In the little gate-house I met Mr. Bradlaugh, Mrs. Besant, and my wife. Colonel Milman wished us good-bye, the gate opened, and a mighty shout broke from the huge crowd outside. From all parts of London they had wended in the early morning to greet me, and there they stood in their thousands. Yet I felt rather sad than elated. The world was so full of wrong, though the hearts of those men and women beat so true!

As our open carriage crawled through the dense crowd I saw men's lips twitching and women shedding tears. They crowded round us, eager for a shake of the hand, a word, a look. At length we got free, and drove towards the Hall of Science, followed by a procession of brakes and other vehicles over half a mile long.

There was a public breakfast, at which hundreds sat down. I took a cup of tea, but ate nothing. After a long imprisonment I could not trust my stomach, and I had to make a speech.

After Mr. Bradlaugh, Mrs. Besant and the Rev. W. Sharman (secretary of the Society for the Repeal of the Blasphemy Laws), had made speeches, which I should blush to transcribe, I rose to respond. It was a ticklish moment. But I found I had a voice still, and the words came readily enough. Concluding my address I said: "I thank you for your greeting. I am not played out. I am thinner. The doctor told me I had lost two stone, and I believe it. But after all I do not think the ship's timbers are much injured. The rogues ran me aground, but they never made me haul down the flag. Now I am floated again I mean to let the old flag stream out on the wind as of yore. I mean to join the rest of our fleet in fighting the pirates and slavers on the high seas of thought."

An hour afterwards my feet were on my own fender. I was home again. What a delicious sensation after twelve months in a prison cell!

Friends prescribed a rest at the seaside for me, but I felt that the best tonic was work. In less than three days I settled everything. I resumed the editorship of the Freethinker at once, and began filling up my list of engagements. On meeting the Committee, who had managed our affairs in our absence, I found everything in perfect order, besides a considerable profit at the banker's. Messrs. A. Hilditch, R. O. Smith, J., Grout and G. Standring had given ungrudgingly of their time; Mr. C. Herbert, acting as treasurer, had kept the accounts with painstaking precision; and Mrs. Besant had proved how a woman could take the lead of men. Nor must I forget Mr. Robert Forder, the Secretary of the National Secular Society, who acted as shopman at our publishing office, and sustained the business by his assiduity. I had also to thank Dr. Aveling for his interim editorship of the Freethinker, and the admirable manner in which he had conducted Progress.

The first number of the Freethinker under my fresh editorship appeared on the following Thursday. In concluding my introductory address I said:

> "I promise the readers of the Freethinker that they shall,
> so far as my powers avail, find no diminution in the vigor and
> vivacity of its attacks on the shams and superstitions of our age.
> Not only the writer's pen, but the artist's pencil, shall be busy

in this good work; and the absurdities of faith shall, if possible, be slain with laughter. Priests and fools are, as Goldsmith said, the two classes who dread ridicule, and we are pledged to an implacable war with both."

The artist's pencil! Yes, I had resolved to repeat what I was punished for. I left written instructions against the publication of Comic Bible Sketches in the Freethinker during my imprisonment; but although I would not impose the risk on others, I was determined to face it myself. A fortnight after my release the Sketches were resumed, and they have been continued ever since. My reasons for this decision were expressed at a public banquet in the Hall of Science on March 12. I then said:

> "Mr. Bradlaugh has said that the Freethought party—which no one will dispute his right to speak for—looks to me, among others, after my imprisonment, to maintain with dignity whatever position I have won. I hope I shall not disappoint the expectation. But I should like it to be clearly understood that I consider the most dignified attitude for a man who has just left gaol after suffering a cruel and unjust sentence, for no crime except that of thinking and speaking freely, is to stand again for the same right he exercised before, to pursue the very policy for which he was attacked, precisely because he was attacked, and to flinch no hair's breadth from the line he pursued before, at least until the opposition resorts to suasion instead of force, and tries to win by criticism what it will never win by the gaol. It is my intention to-morrow morning to drive to the West of London, and to leave the first copy of this week's Freethinker pulled from the press at Judge North's house with my compliments and my card."

Prolonged applause greeted this announcement, and I kept my word. Judge North had the first copy of the re-illustrated Freethinker and I hope he relished. At any rate, it showed him, as John Bright says, that "force is no remedy."

At the banquet I refer to I was presented with a purse of gold, in common with Mr. Ramsey, and an Illuminated Address, which ran as follows:

> "To GEORGE WILLIAM FOOTE, Vice-President of the National Secular
> Society, who suffered for twelve months in Holloway Gaol for the so-called offence of Blasphemy.

"In offering you on your release this illuminated address, and the accompanying purse of gold, we do not seek to give you recompense for the sufferings and insults which have been heaped upon you. We bring them only as a symbol of our thanks to you—thanks, because, on your trial, you spoke nobly for the right of free speech on religious questions; thanks, because you bore, without a sign of flinching, a sentence at once cruel and unjust; thanks, because you have carried on our days the traditions of a Freethought faithful in the prison as on the platform.

"Signed on behalf of the National Secular Society
C. BRADLAUGH, President.
R. FORDER, Secretary."

Greatly also did I value the greeting I received, with my two fellow prisoners, from the working men of East London. At a crowded meeting in the large hall of the Haggerston Road Club, attended by representatives of other associations, I was presented with the following address:

"The Political Council of the Borough of Hackney Workmen's Club present this testimonial to George William Foote as a token of admiration of the courage displayed by him in the advocacy of free speech, and in sympathy for the sufferings endured during twelve months' imprisonment for the same under barbarous laws unfitted for the spirit of a free people.

"Signed on behalf of the Council
ALFRED PIKE, President.
CHAS. KNIGHT, Secretary."

The largest audience that ever assembled at the Hall of Science listened to my first lecture, at which Mr. Bradlaugh presided, two days after my release. Seventeen hundred people crowded into a room that seats nine hundred, and as many were unable to gain admission. Similar welcomes awaited me in the provinces; and ever since my audiences, as well as the sale of my journal and writings, have been far larger than before my imprisonment. Hundreds of people, as they have told me, have been converted to Freethought by my sufferings, my lectures, and my pamphlets. I hope Judge North is satisfied.

To prevent a break-down in case of another prosecution, Mr. Ramsey and I clubbed our resources, and purchased printing plant and machinery, so that the production of the Freethinker and other "blasphemous" literature might be done under our own root. The bigots had proved themselves unable to intimidate us, and as we were no longer at the mercy of printers they gave up the idea of molesting us. May Freethinkers ever act in this spirit, and be true to the great traditions of our cause!

FINIS

www.ingramcontent.com/pod-product-compliance
Lightning Source LLC
Chambersburg PA
CBHW011255040426
42453CB00015B/2415